Clever Quarters, Too

D0607900

Clever Quarters, Too

MORE QUILTS FROM FAT QUARTERS

Susan Teegarden Dissmore

Martingale®
& COMPANY

CREDITS

President: Nancy J. Martin
CEO: Daniel J. Martin
COO: Tom Wierzbicki
Publisher: Jane Hamada
Editorial Director: Mary V. Green
Managing Editor: Tina Cook
Technical Editor: Laurie Baker
Copy Editor: Melissa Bryan
Design Director: Stan Green
Illustrator: Laurel Strand
Text Designer: Trina Craig
Cover Designer: Stan Green
Photographer: Brent Kane

Clever Quarters, Too: More Quilts from Fat Quarters
© 2006 by Susan Teegarden Dissmore

That Patchwork Place® is an imprint of
Martingale & Company®.

Martingale & Company
20205 144th Ave. NE
Woodinville, WA 98072-8478
www.martingale-pub.com

Printed in China
11 10 09 08 07   8 7 6 5 4 3 2

No part of this product may be reproduced in any form, unless otherwise stated, in which case reproduction is limited to the use of the purchaser. The written instructions, photographs, designs, projects, and patterns are intended for the personal, noncommercial use of the retail purchaser and are under federal copyright laws; they are not to be reproduced by any electronic, mechanical, or other means, including informational storage or retrieval systems, for commercial use. Permission is granted to photocopy patterns for the personal use of the retail purchaser.

The information in this book is presented in good faith, but no warranty is given nor results guaranteed. Since Martingale & Company has no control over choice of materials or procedures, the company assumes no responsibility for the use of this information.

MISSION STATEMENT

Dedicated to providing quality products and service to inspire creativity.

Library of Congress Cataloging-in-Publication Data
Library of Congress Control Number: 2006019495

ISBN-13: 978-1-56477-627-3
ISBN-10: 1-56477-627-1

DEDICATION

To Kitty Bailey, Mary Ann Gobat, Terry Crane, and Stephanie Swensson, who kept the shop fires burning over the last two years while I spent time writing and sewing.

ACKNOWLEDGMENTS

My husband deserves a huge pat on the back for supporting every effort I've made in the quilting business. Disagreements may have been lodged, but never enforced, allowing the continued pursuit of my dream. The chase hasn't always been easy; owning a quilt shop in conjunction with writing quiltmaking books has left very little spare time in my life for other interests.

Similarly, if it weren't for my hard-working, dedicated staff, I would not have been able to create the multitude of quilts for this book. The shop continued to operate without my presence as the staff motivated and inspired my customers. The staff's help was priceless!

I love to create quilt tops, but quilting them is a tedious chore. The thread artistry of Eileen Peacher and Sue Gantt on a long-arm quilting machine turns my simple tops into marvelous works of art. Their efforts are greatly appreciated. I would not be able to finish a quiltmaking book without them.

Thank you to Moda Fabrics for the inspiration to make the quilt "Summer by the Sea" from their Seaside Rose fabric collection, and also for allowing me to modify their design to showcase the versatility of fat quarters.

Thanks to the helpful staff at Martingale & Company. There is always something new to learn about publishing a book, and they are always there to lend a guiding hand.

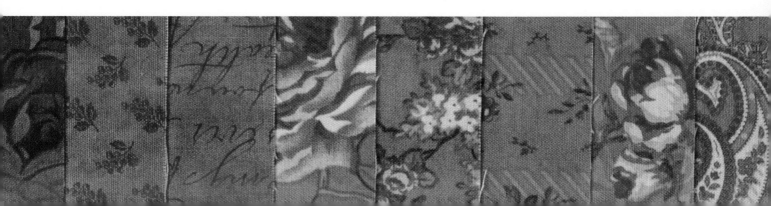

Contents

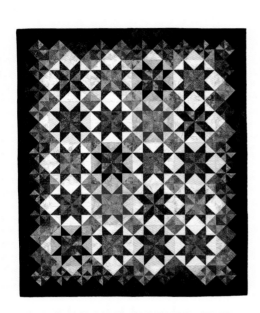

Introduction

Fat quarters are like quilter's candy. The colorful fabrics remind me of jelly beans in a jar enticing you to grab a handful (one is never enough). Typically presented in neatly folded stacks tied with pretty ribbon or coordinated by color families in baskets and bins, these fabric gems are impossible to ignore.

My favorite quilts are traditional designs composed of a multitude of fabrics; in other words, scrap quilts. The easiest way I have found to collect fabrics for a scrap quilt is through the use of fat quarters. Once I have a nice-sized collection, the question then becomes how to adapt the fabrics into a fat-quarter-friendly quilt. One answer is to simply choose a design, convert each listed amount of yardage into quarter-yard increments, and apply that result to each element of the design.

For me, however, creating a scrap quilt requires a blank canvas prepared for painting a work of art with fat quarters used as the palette. Selecting just the right pieces for the palette is the first challenge faced. Because many fabric companies now offer entire collections in fat-quarter form, choosing a coordinated collection of fabrics for the palette has been made easier through the use of those bundles. If pre-bundled collections aren't available to you, selecting fat quarters individually is always an option.

After the preliminary palette is chosen, the next step is to find just the right design. During the design process, color placement may be altered and fabrics may be added (or eliminated) while keeping in mind that each piece must be just one fat quarter. Once the design is colored and the pieces are cut and sewn, anticipation soars to view the final result.

In my first fat-quarter book, *Clever Quarters*, the goal was to create quilt tops that used fat quarters exclusively—no larger cuts allowed. In this book, you'll find that I have loosened those restrictions when creating borders. What if you can't find six dark red fat quarters of similar color and value, but you've found one piece of fabric that you love? (That was my dilemma in the quilt on page 76, "Ruby's Golden Railroad.") Consider purchasing the full amount of required yardage instead of individual fat quarters. Larger cuts can be included successfully without spoiling the effect of the scrappy quilt—especially in an outer border. By isolating one aspect of the quilt (such as the border), you can devote more time to selecting just the right fat quarters for the center of the quilt. Flexibility is the key!

Using more than one fat quarter of the same print is also allowed. Just because individual quantities of fat quarters are listed doesn't mean you can't duplicate them. I successfully duplicated prints in several of the quilts, and I have noted these instances in the materials lists of the relevant projects.

In this fast-paced world, many desire instant results. Although the designs in this book are relatively easy, choosing just the right fabrics for each project will require an adequate amount of planning and thought. But once you have jumped that hurdle, you are well on your way to creating your own quilt masterpiece. You'll have the satisfaction of a job well done and the rewards will last a lifetime.

Let's Talk about Fat Quarters

Several months passed after the opening of my quilt shop before I discovered the magic of fat quarters. What I learned early on was that a fat quarter is simply a half yard that has been cut in half on the fold, typically yielding a piece measuring 18" x 21". A fat quarter has the same amount of area as a standard quarter-yard cut that measures 9" x 42", but the 18" width allows for cutting larger pieces. Because fat quarters are usually precut, they are easier to handle when you need lots of them. Fat quarters are much lighter than bolts of fabric!

Although visualizing a quilt shop without an ample supply of fat quarters may be difficult, the possibility exists. If your favorite quilt shop doesn't cut or carry them, consider purchasing half-yard pieces to make your own fat quarters. (See the tip at right.) That way you'll have two—one for now and one for your fabric library!

Not all fat quarters are created equal. The standard width of quiltmaking fabric from selvage to selvage is 42". When a half-yard piece is cut in half along the fold, the resulting two pieces should be 18" x 21" each. This measurement will vary when the yardage width is more or less than the standard 42" and the half yard itself is cut more or less than 18". Always check the measurements of your fat quarters before you start. Should you come up short, simply add another fat quarter.

I prewash every piece of fabric before I use it in any quilt project. Prewashing adds another alteration to the final dimension of your fat quarter. It's possible to lose as much as ½" on each side, reducing the dimension to 17" x 20". Once you straighten that fat quarter, the width will shrink even more. The projects in this book assume that the final width of your fat quarter is 17" and the length is 20" (although 21" is used in the cutting lists).

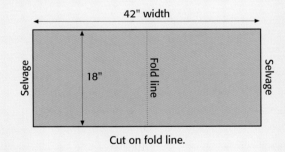

CLEVER TIP

Making Your Own Fat Quarters

To convert a half yard into two fat quarters, simply fold the fabric in half and match the selvage edges. Make a crease along the fold of the fabric. Open up the fabric and cut on the fold with a rotary cutter or scissors. You now have two pieces of fabric that measure approximately 18" x 21".

42" width

Selvage | 18" | Fold line | Selvage

Cut on fold line.

CHOOSING FAT QUARTERS

Listed with each project is the quantity of fat quarters required for each quilt. Some of the projects use as few as 5 fat quarters, while several require 30 or more. Selecting so many fat quarters may feel like a daunting task. To help you with possible choices, a photo of the fabrics used for each project (except "Shining Star Place Mats" on page 87) is also included. Because fabric lines are short-lived, the exact fabrics I used may no longer be available. Use the photos as inspiration to find comparable substitutes. If the fabrics shown don't appeal to you, spend time reviewing the materials list to determine the types of colors, values, and prints needed to create your own unique palette.

Lacking a background in art and color theory, I consider myself lucky to possess a natural gift for choosing color. This section will take you through my personal process of choosing fabrics, but won't provide an in-depth discussion of color theory. If my personal guidelines don't offer enough assistance or you want to learn more, consider purchasing a book devoted to the subject of color. A color wheel or color tool may also be helpful.

Many of the quilts in this book were created from a prebundled collection of fat quarters, to which I added or deleted pieces when necessary. If you've been collecting coordinated bundles, here is your chance to pull out your favorite one. If you are starting from scratch, save time by first trying to find a coordinated stack of fat quarters at your local quilt shop. If you can't find just the right group, start collecting individual fat quarters (or half yards) in your favorite colors and in various prints, including plaids and stripes, to build your fabric library.

When choosing individual fat quarters, start with your favorite color first, disregarding its value or scale. Find that chosen color on a color wheel and work clockwise until you have gathered at least one fabric in each color family that looks good next to your first choice. The quantity of coordinates is up to you. Once you have done that, it's time to think about the value and scale.

Value is determined by the lightness or darkness of a fabric. A light fabric could be white, ivory, beige, or tan with (or without) any other color added to the print. A dark value is simply that—dark—and a medium value falls somewhere between the light and the dark. Values can vary depending on the lightness or darkness of the fabrics placed next to them.

Expanding on your first choices and following

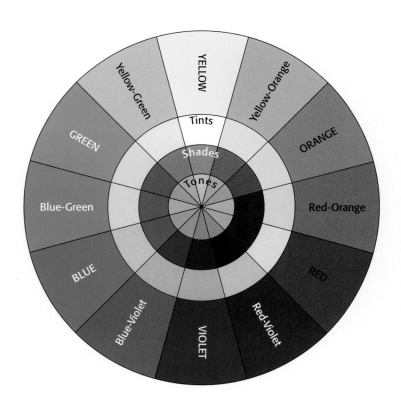

the same color-wheel concept, choose coordinating fabrics that are lighter, between, or darker than the original ones. Stack them in order of your perception of light to dark. Use a transparent value finder to see if your perception is correct. Value can also be tested by standing back at least 10 feet from the fabric and squinting. Squinting helps you see variations in value more easily.

CLEVER TIP

Value Finders

Value finders are transparent acrylic rectangles colored in green or red. When we view fabrics through them, value finders remove the color and reveal only the values. Having both red and green value finders on hand is helpful because the red value finder won't work with red fabrics, and the green value finder won't work with green fabrics. Value finders can be purchased at quilt shops or through catalogs.

Scale refers to the size of the print on a fabric. After testing the value, examine your selections to see how many of the prints vary in size. A mix of various scales in a quilt not only adds movement, but also keeps the eye interested. If your collection lacks a variety of scale, rethink your choices with the following guidelines.

I consider a large-scale print one with images greater than 4" in diameter, and a medium scale somewhere between 2" and 4" in diameter. These prints are typically used as focal points within a block. "A Bouquet for You" on page 20 uses a large-scale floral print, whereas "Finally Fall" on page 55 uses several medium-scale leaf prints. A small-scale print has scattered images that are, naturally, smaller than a medium-scale print. Many quilters refer to these small prints as calicoes.

I also use lots of tone-on-tone prints in my quilts. A tone-on-tone print will read as a solid color, but it creates the movement and interest that I like in a quilt. I use both small-scale and tone-on-tone prints to accent the large- and medium-scale pieces, and I also like to include plaid or striped accents from time to time as a fun alternative. I prefer not to use true solids; I feel they tend to stop the eye from moving across the quilt.

Combining all of the previously discussed elements will create your palette. Palettes are collections of fabrics that vary in scale and value and are colored in various tints, shades, and tones of a pure color. Consider the brightest, clearest fabric your pure color. Adding white to a pure color will create a pastel tint; adding black creates a deep, warm shade; and adding gray creates a soft, subtle tone.

All the quilts in this book can be created with any color palette you desire. If you don't like the palette I have chosen for a project, change it to reflect your own unique color style or preference. Treat these projects as a testing ground—a way to experiment with new combinations of color and print. I promise that it will be fun and rewarding, and it will become easier as you practice.

PREPARING FAT QUARTERS

As I mentioned, I prewash all fabrics prior to their use. Fabrics will shrink at different rates and sometimes lose color. By prewashing, you may prevent a disaster later on. Wash your fabrics on the gentle cycle with like colors and remove them from the dryer while they are still damp. Press them immediately to remove wrinkles. If desired, add spray sizing or starch when you press to restore the body and crispness lost during the washing process. The sizing or starch will make it easier to control your fabrics while cutting, sewing, and pressing seam allowances.

Once your fat quarter is prewashed, you may have only a 17" x 20" piece of usable fabric. Although all cross-grain cuts in the projects have been listed as 21" wide, the yardage requirements have been calculated based on a usable width of 20" to ensure you'll have adequate fabric to complete the project.

Quiltmaking Basics

Whether you are a seasoned quilter or new to the art, spend a little time reviewing this section. It offers tips and techniques essential to your success.

TOOLS AND SUPPLIES

My advice to beginning quilters is to invest in the best-quality tools and supplies they can afford. This investment will make quilting easier and more accurate; both the process of making a quilt and the end result will be successful and rewarding.

SEWING MACHINE

A fancy sewing machine isn't necessary for general quiltmaking, but a machine in top-notch working order is essential. Treat your machine like your best friend. After every project, remove any lint that may have accumulated and change the needle. To keep your machine in good working order, have it serviced periodically by a trained professional.

The stitch quality on your machine is also important. You want your stitch to be even on both sides of the fabric—not too tight or too loose. A tight tension may cause puckering; a loose tension will cause your stitch to come apart.

ROTARY-CUTTING TOOLS

A sharp rotary cutter has become a necessary tool for quiltmaking. With care, your rotary blade should last quite a while before requiring replacement. Just be careful not to nick the blade by cutting over pins or your ruler. When not in use, keep the blade closed. These blades are extremely sharp and dangerous.

I use clear acrylic rulers with ⅛" markings. When cutting strips from a fat quarter, I find that a 6" x 12" ruler works the best; however, a ruler that measures 6" x 24" would work as well. I use square rulers for cutting squares and trimming up blocks or pieces. The square ruler sizes I prefer are 6½", 8", 9½", and 12½". If you need to purchase these and don't want to invest in all of them right away, start with the larger ones first.

In addition to the rotary cutter and acrylic rulers, you'll need a self-healing mat specifically for use with a rotary cutter. At the minimum, the mat should measure 18" x 24". Be sure to store your mat in a cool space where it can be kept flat. Once a mat is warped, it cannot be reshaped.

THREAD

Use high-quality, long-staple cotton thread when stitching quilts. If the thread looks fuzzy on the spool, it is a sign of a short-staple thread that should be avoided. Light gray, beige, or white threads will work for piecing most quilt tops. For machine quilting, choose a thread color that coordinates with the top and/or backing fabric.

OTHER BASIC SEWING SUPPLIES

You'll also need basic sewing supplies, including scissors for cutting thread, a seam ripper, straight pins (I prefer sharp, glass-head straight pins because the head is easy to grab and won't melt if touched by an iron), and basic sewing-machine needles. Size 80/12 universal machine needles work well for piecing. For machine quilting, purchase needles specifically for that purpose. Template plastic is also handy for selective cutting, which will be discussed on page 14.

ROTARY CUTTING

Before you begin to cut strips from your fat quarters, you'll need to straighten the edges of the fabric.

1. Fold your fat quarter in half from the one remaining selvage edge to the cut edge. Keeping the edges together, hold your fabric out in front of you. Let the fabric hang freely. Move the edges of the fabric until it hangs wrinkle-free. Carefully lay the folded fabric on your cutting mat.

2. Align the edge of a square ruler along the folded edge. Place a 6" x 12" (or 6" x 24") ruler to the left of the square ruler and keep the ruler edges together. Remove the square ruler and cut away a small portion of the left side of the fabric. (If you are left-handed, reverse this process.) You now have a clean, straight edge from which to cut strips.

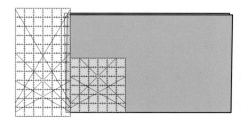

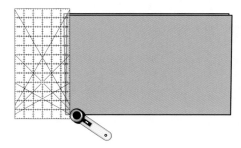

3. To cut strips, move the 6" x 12" ruler to the right, matching the ruler line for the desired width to the freshly cut edges. Cut a strip. Repeat until you have the desired number of strips.

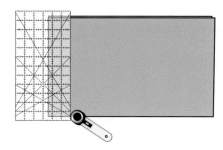

4. To cut squares from the strips, straighten one end of the strip first. Align the left side (or right side, if you're left-handed) of the strip with the desired line on the ruler. This measurement should match the strip width. Cut the desired number of squares from the strips.

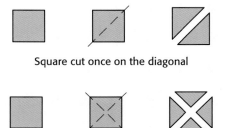

Cut squares from a strip.

5. The squares can then be left intact, cut in half diagonally once, or cut in half diagonally twice, as needed.

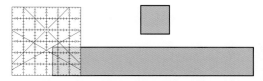

Square cut once on the diagonal

Square cut twice on the diagonal

6. To cut rectangles, first cut a strip with a width equal to the short dimension of the desired rectangle. Straighten one end of the strip; then align the ruler to the left side (or right side if you're left-handed) of the strip and match the required length of the rectangle. Cut the desired number of rectangles from the strip. For instance, if you need rectangles that measure 2½" x 4½", you would cut a 2½"-wide strip, and then cut the strip into 4½"-long segments.

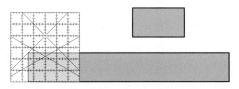

Cut rectangles from a strip.

Selective Cutting

Once in a while you may need to selectively cut a desired motif from your fat quarter. I recommend using translucent template plastic to accurately center and cut the motif.

1. Cut a piece of template plastic to the finished size of the shape desired. Draw an X on the template plastic, with lines connecting opposite corners and crossing at the center.

2. Place the template plastic on your fabric and move it around until you have centered the desired motif to your satisfaction. Using a ruler and rotary cutter, cut ¼" beyond each side of the template plastic. Place your ruler carefully over the template plastic when cutting. You may want to add temporary spray adhesive or sandpaper dots to the back of the template plastic to keep it from slipping while you are cutting.

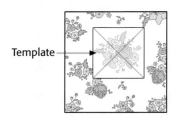

Template →

CLEVER TIP

Reusable Templates

Squares of template plastic are reusable. Whenever you cut a square of a new size, write the dimensions on the template with a permanent marker. Store all your templates together in an envelope for quick access in the future.

MACHINE PIECING

Grab a comfortable chair and get an iron and ironing board ready. It's time to start piecing your quilt.

Maintaining the ¼" Seam

All the cutting instructions in this book include a ¼"-wide seam allowance. To achieve the best results in machine piecing, maintain a straight, scant ¼" seam allowance throughout the project. Every aspect of your quilt top will be affected if you don't maintain that seam allowance.

What is a straight, scant ¼" seam allowance? A scant seam allowance is at least one to two threads smaller than an actual ¼". This allows for the space that is taken up by the thread and fabric when you press the seam allowance to one side. To keep the seam straight, I highly recommend the use of a ¼" machine presser foot. If you don't have a foot available, use an adhesive product such as ¼"-wide masking tape or moleskin that can be attached to the bed of your machine (not on the feed dogs). Once you have attached the foot or adhesive guide, check for accuracy by holding a ruler next to the raw edge of your fabric. The thread should be just inside the ¼" line of your ruler. Adjust the position of your needle or adhesive guide until you have achieved the desired seam-allowance width.

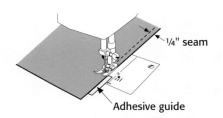

¼" seam

Adhesive guide

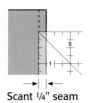

Scant ¼" seam

Chain Piecing

Chain piecing is a process of feeding layered pairs of triangles, strips, or patches through your sewing machine one after another. It is fast and efficient,

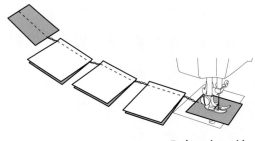

End sewing with a scrap of fabric.

eliminating the need to continually snip threads and thread tails. Once you have finished a chain-pieced set, feed a small piece of scrap fabric through the machine as the last piece. Snip your threads and transfer the separate pieces to your pressing surface.

SEWING STRIP SETS

Throughout this book you'll be instructed to sew strip sets. A strip set consists of two or more strips sewn together along their long edges. They can then be crosscut and used alone (Rail Fence blocks) or sewn to other crosscut units to make blocks or components of blocks (Four Patch blocks). On occasion, you may be instructed to "unsew" or remove parts of strip sets with a seam ripper to obtain a required number of units.

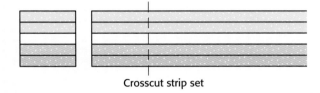

Crosscut strip set

PRESSING

Pressing after sewing each seam helps ensure the accuracy of your piecing. Although I have included some pressing instructions with each project, the rule of thumb is to press seam allowances to one side, usually toward the darker fabric. Occasionally, you may need to press a seam allowance open to eliminate bulk. Press with a hot, dry iron set for cotton. Although I like a little steam, it can cause stretching. Be careful if you choose to apply steam to your pieces.

As you press, try to plan ahead so you'll have opposing seam allowances within your quilt blocks and rows of your quilt top. By doing this, you'll have seams that butt up against each other, allowing you to match seam intersections perfectly. On occasion, seams don't butt up against each other and can't be re-pressed. If this happens, pin the seams at the intersection and sew through the extra bulk carefully.

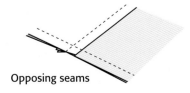

Opposing seams

WORKING WITH TRIANGLES

Several of the blocks featured in this book use triangles. Because most of my quilts are scrappy, I usually cut triangles from squares and sew them back together individually. Extra care must be taken when sewing triangles because the center cut will be on the bias. Because bias tends to stretch, let your machine's feed dogs do all the work when sewing triangles. Triangles can be sewn into half-square-triangle units, quarter-square-triangle units, or flying-geese units.

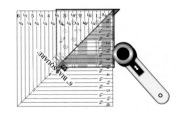

CLEVER TIP

Making Triangle Units

There are lots of ways to cut and sew half-square-triangle and quarter-square-triangle units. Most often, I choose to cut my triangles separately and sew them individually. If you prefer a different method, review your favorite assembly instructions for that technique before cutting the pieces for the triangle units. It's possible that you'll need to adapt the cutting instructions to your particular method.

SQUARING UP BLOCKS

When stitching components of blocks, I press and trim as I go. If a block is made up of half-square triangles, for instance, I will press the seam allowance and trim the triangle unit to the desired unfinished size, even if just a few threads need to be cut away. This also removes any "dog-ears" that extend beyond the piece and can cause extra bulk in the seam. Trimming as you go will ensure that the finished block will be nearly perfect when the pieces are sewn together.

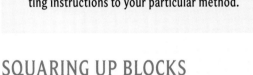

After stitching all the patches of your quilt blocks together, press and trim again if needed. Use a large square ruler to measure the blocks and make sure they are the desired size plus a ¼" seam allowance on each edge. For example, if you are making 12" blocks, they should all measure 12½" before you sew them together. Be consistent with this step, making sure that all your blocks are the same measurement. If your blocks aren't the required size, you'll need to adjust all other components of the quilt accordingly.

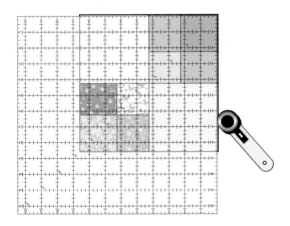

SETTING BLOCKS TOGETHER

Blocks are typically arranged in rows before being sewn together. Pin the blocks together at intersections to make sure that your seams line up properly. Stitch the blocks together row by row and press all the seam allowances within a row in one direction (unless instructed otherwise). Prior to stitching the rows together, press seam allowances in opposite directions from row to row for easier matching. Stitch the rows together.

ADDING PIECED BORDERS

Every quilt in this book has a pieced outer border, allowing you to utilize your fat quarters to their fullest potential. Attaching a pieced outer border to your quilt top may require some re-pressing and seam-allowance adjustments. When you are ready to attach your border units to the quilt top, follow the guidance in the assembly instructions to place the borders right sides together and pin at seam intersections. Once pinned, you can determine whether a seam allowance needs to be re-pressed or adjusted.

CLEVER TIP

Re-pressing
Border Seam Allowances

Border-unit seam allowances occasionally need to be re-pressed in the opposite direction of the quilt top so that seams will butt up against each other. First press the seam allowance flat as it was when stitched, and then press to the opposite side.

If the quilt top is slightly larger than the border strip (or vice versa), ease the bigger piece to match the smaller piece when stitching. To do this, place the longer of the two pieces (either the quilt top or border strip) on the bed of your machine, with the wrong side of the shorter piece facing you. This allows the feed dogs to do their job; they will move the lower layer along at a slightly faster speed than the top layer. Always handle border strips carefully to avoid stretching. Remove pins as you sew rather than sewing over them, so that they don't nick and dull the machine needle.

Easing pieced border onto quilt top

Because the intent of this book is to use fat quarters, straight-grain borders were not added to the pieced borders. It is possible, however, to add straight-grain borders to some of the quilts without adversely affecting the design. Yardage for straight-grain borders hasn't been included in the materials lists and would need to be calculated based on the measurement of the quilt top.

CLEVER TIP

Resizing Pieced Border Units

If your border unit is too large, increase the seam allowances by just a thread or two. If the border unit is too small, reduce seam allowances by "unsewing" and resewing with a slightly smaller seam allowance until you achieve a good fit.

FINISHING YOUR QUILT

Once your quilt top is complete, you need to decide how you would like to finish it. Are you planning to stitch in the ditch, or will you need to mark the quilting designs on your quilt top? Although marking isn't necessary for stitching in the ditch and some free-motion quilting, a complex design may need to be marked on the quilt top before it is layered with batting and backing.

Using 42"-wide fabric, most quilts in this book will require a pieced backing. Prewash and remove all selvage edges from your backing fabric before you sew the pieces together. The backing and batting should extend 2" to 4" beyond the finished quilt top on all sides.

ASSEMBLING THE QUILT SANDWICH

The next step is to make the quilt sandwich, which consists of the backing, batting, and quilt top. Your batting choice will hinge on whether you choose to machine or hand quilt. Check with your local quilt shop to determine the perfect batting for your project.

1. Lay the backing fabric, wrong side up, on a smooth, clean surface. Keep the backing fabric taut and wrinkle-free but not stretched. Secure the backing to the surface with masking tape or binder clips.

2. Lay the batting over the backing. Starting from the center, smooth out the batting until there are no wrinkles.

3. Lay the quilt top, right side up, over the batting. Starting from the center, smooth out the quilt top over the batting.

4. Pin or hand baste the layers together. Because I machine quilt, I use #1 safety pins for basting large quilts and basting spray for small quilts. Begin pinning in the center of the quilt and work toward the outer edges. The placement of the pins will depend on the type of machine quilting you plan to do, but place them no more than 3" apart. If you use a basting spray, follow the instructions included with the product.

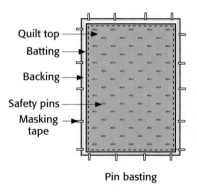

Quilt top
Batting
Backing
Safety pins
Masking tape

Pin basting

5. If you plan to hand quilt, thread basting is a better choice. Sew a large grid of stitches using a cotton thread. Begin in the center of the quilt and stitch lines about 4" to 6" apart in all directions. Make the final stitches around the outer edges of the quilt.

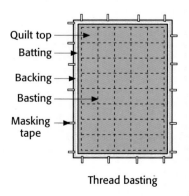

Quilt top
Batting
Backing
Basting
Masking tape

Thread basting

6. Machine or hand quilt as desired.

BINDING

Binding is the final step in completing your quilt. I cut binding strips on the cross grain, 2½" x 42", to make a ½"-wide finished binding. For a narrower binding, cut narrower strips.

1. Cut enough strips to go around the edges of your quilt, with an extra 12" for turning corners and joining ends. Sew the strips together with diagonal seams, forming one continuous strip. Trim the seam allowances to ¼". Press the seam allowances open to minimize bulk.

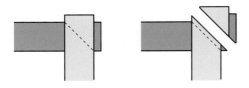

2. Press the binding strip in half lengthwise with the wrong sides together.

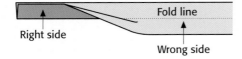

3. Position the binding all the way around the quilt, making sure that none of the seams fall at the corners of the quilt.

4. Leaving an 8" to 10" tail at the beginning, sew the binding to the quilt top with a ¼" seam allowance. Use a walking foot or dual-feed mechanism to help feed all the layers through the machine evenly.

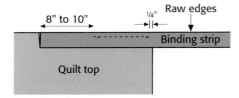

5. When you approach a corner, stop ¼" from it. Backstitch and remove the quilt from the machine. Turn the quilt so that you'll be stitching down the next side. Fold the binding up at a 45° angle so the binding raw edges are parallel to the side of the quilt. Then fold the strip down so that the fold is parallel to the top edge of the quilt and the raw edges are aligned with the side edge of the quilt. Begin sewing from the top with a ¼" seam allowance.

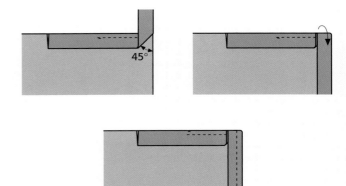

6. Continue in this manner around the quilt, stopping 8" to 10" from where you began stitching. Backstitch and remove the quilt from the machine. Trim the binding so that the beginning and ending tails overlap by 2½". (The overlap should equal the width that you cut your binding strips.)

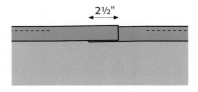

7. Open and place the strips, right sides together, at right angles. Stitch on the diagonal and trim away the excess fabric. Press the seam allowance open. Refold the binding and finish sewing it to the quilt.

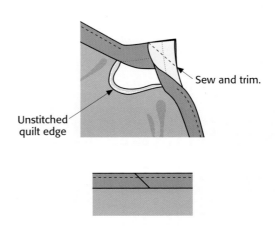

CLEVER TIP

Joining Binding Strips

Before sewing the strips together, fold and press a diagonal seam line on the binding strip. That way, you'll have a guideline to follow when stitching.

8. Fold the binding from the front of the quilt to the back and pin it in place if desired. It should cover the binding stitching line. Whipstitch the folded edge to the back of the quilt, using a thread that matches the binding. Be careful that your stitches don't go through to the front. As you approach the first corner, pull the binding to make sure extra fabric hasn't bunched up. With your thumbnail at the corner, fold over the unstitched binding edge, creating a miter. Secure it with stitches. Repeat for the remaining corners.

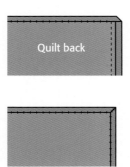

Quilt back

ADDING A LABEL

This step takes only a few minutes and is well worth the effort. Adding a label will document information about your quilt. The label can be elaborate or plain. I like to work with preprinted labels, because they are both decorative and easy to use. With a permanent ink pen, I simply write the name of the quilt, my name, the quilter's name (if applicable), the date it was completed, and the place where it was completed. I fold under the edges of the label and just whipstitch it into place. It's that simple.

A Bouquet for You

Designed, sewn, and quilted by Susan Dissmore, 2004.

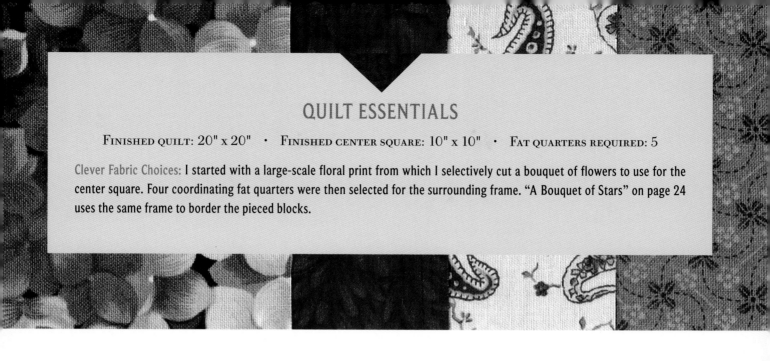

FINISHED QUILT: 20" x 20" • FINISHED CENTER SQUARE: 10" x 10" • FAT QUARTERS REQUIRED: 5

Clever Fabric Choices: I started with a large-scale floral print from which I selectively cut a bouquet of flowers to use for the center square. Four coordinating fat quarters were then selected for the surrounding frame. "A Bouquet of Stars" on page 24 uses the same frame to border the pieced blocks.

MATERIALS

Yardages are based on 42"-wide fabric.

- ✦ 1 fat quarter of large-scale floral print for center square
- ✦ 1 fat quarter of pink floral print for center square and frame
- ✦ 1 fat quarter of burgundy print for frame
- ✦ 1 fat quarter of beige print for frame
- ✦ 1 fat quarter of green print for frame
- ✦ ⅜ yard of fabric for binding
- ✦ ¾ yard of fabric for backing
- ✦ 26" x 26" piece of batting

CUTTING

All measurements include ¼" seam allowances.

From the large-scale floral print, selectively cut:
- ✦ 1 square, 10½" x 10½"

From the pink floral print, cut:
- ✦ 1 square, 6¼" x 6¼"; cut the square in half diagonally twice to yield 4 triangles
- ✦ 8 squares, 3" x 3"

From the burgundy print, cut:
- ✦ 1 square, 6¼" x 6¼"; cut the square in half diagonally twice to yield 4 triangles
- ✦ 2 strips, 3⅜" x 21". Cut the strips into 8 squares, 3⅜" x 3⅜"; cut the squares in half diagonally once to yield 16 triangles.

From the beige print, cut:
- ✦ 1 strip, 6¼" x 21". Cut the strip into 2 squares, 6¼" x 6¼"; cut the squares in half diagonally twice to yield 8 triangles.
- ✦ 2 strips, 3⅜" x 21". Cut the strips into 8 squares, 3⅜" x 3⅜"; cut the squares in half diagonally once to yield 16 triangles.
- ✦ 4 squares, 3" x 3"

From the green print, cut:
- ✦ 2 strips, 3⅜" x 21". Cut the strips into 8 squares, 3⅜" x 3⅜"; cut the squares in half diagonally once to yield 16 triangles.

ASSEMBLY

1. With right sides together, place a pink floral square on one corner of the large-scale floral square. Draw a diagonal line through the 3" square as shown and stitch on the line. Leaving a ¼" seam allowance, trim away the excess fabric. Press the seam allowance toward the pink square. Repeat on each corner.

10½"

Make 1.

2. Using the triangles cut from 3⅜" squares, sew the beige triangles to the burgundy triangles along their longest edges to form half-square-triangle units. Press the seam allowances toward the burgundy triangles and trim the dog-ears.

3"

Make 8.

3. Sew the remaining triangles cut from 3⅜" squares to each short side of the triangles cut from 6¼" squares to make flying-geese units in the color combinations shown. Press the seam allowances toward the smaller triangles and trim the dog-ears.

5½"

3"

Make 4.

Make 4.   Make 8.

4. Sew the units from steps 2 and 3, the beige squares, and the remaining pink floral squares together into borders as shown. Press the seam allowances as indicated.

5. Referring to the quilt assembly diagram, sew the side inner borders to the center square as shown. Press the seam allowances toward the center square. Sew the top and bottom inner borders to the center square as shown. Press the seam allowances toward the center square. Repeat to sew the outer borders to the quilt top. Press the seam allowances toward the center square.

Quilt assembly

6. Quilt as desired and bind. Refer to "Finishing Your Quilt" on page 17 for details if needed.

Side inner border.
Make 2.

Side outer border.
Make 2.

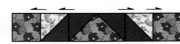

Top/bottom inner border.
Make 2.

Top/bottom outer border.
Make 2.

Size Options

One big block is perfect if you're making a quick gift, but what if you want a larger quilt? The chart that follows lists yardage and cutting instructions for a 4-, 6-, or 12-block quilt. To cut the necessary pieces, refer to "Squares to Cut" for the quantity and "Second Cut" for the shape. Then simply follow the steps of the preceding assembly instructions and repeat until you have stitched the desired amount of blocks. You can choose to substitute the center square with any theme print, floral print, or pieced block having a *finished* size of 10". "A Bouquet of Stars" on page 24 is an example of a large quilt that uses the same frame in an alternate coloration.

Fabric	Piece	Cut Size	Second Cut	Cutting for 4 Blocks		Cutting for 6 Blocks		Cutting for 12 Blocks	
				Squares to Cut	Yardage	Squares to Cut	Yardage	Squares to Cut	Yardage
Pink Floral	A	6¼" x 6¼"	⊠	4	2 fat quarters or ½ yard	6	2 fat quarters or ½ yard	12	4 fat quarters or 1 yard
	B	3" x 3"		32		48		96	
Burgundy	C	3⅜" x 3⅜"	◺	32	3 fat quarters or ¾ yard	48	3 fat quarters or ¾ yard	96	6 fat quarters or 1½ yards
	D	6¼" x 6¼"	⊠	4		6		12	
Beige	E	3⅜" x 3⅜"	◺	32	4 fat quarters or 1 yard	48	5 fat quarters or 1¼ yards	96	9 fat quarters or 2¼ yards
	F	3" x 3"		16		24		48	
	G	6¼" x 6¼"	⊠	8		12		24	
Dark Green	H	3⅜" x 3⅜"	◺	32	2 fat quarters or ½ yard	48	2 fat quarters or ½ yard	96	4 fat quarters or 1 yard

A Bouquet of Stars

Designed and sewn by Susan Dissmore; machine quilted by Eileen Peacher, 2005.

QUILT ESSENTIALS

FINISHED QUILT: 80" x 100" · FINISHED BLOCK: 10" x 10" · FAT QUARTERS REQUIRED: 30

Clever Fabric Choices: A red-and-blue floral print was selected as the main print and used in both the center of each block and the outer border. Coordinating colors of blue, green, and red were used to frame the blocks, and assorted black prints were chosen for the star points created when the framed blocks are sewn together. To maintain the continuity between the blocks, one beige print was used for the background of the blocks and the inner and middle borders. A dark blue print was used in conjunction with the main print to complete the outer border.

MATERIALS

Yardages are based on 42"-wide fabric.

- 3 yards of beige print for blocks, inner border, and middle border
- 4 fat quarters *each* of assorted dark red, dark green, and dark blue prints for blocks (12 total)
- 8 fat quarters of assorted black prints for blocks, inner border, and middle border*
- 7 fat quarters of assorted medium tan prints for blocks, inner border, and middle border
- 1¾ yards of floral print for block centers and outer border
- 1¼ yards of navy tone-on-tone print for outer border
- 3 fat quarters of assorted light tan tone-on-tone prints for blocks
- ⅞ yard of fabric for binding
- 7½ yards of fabric for backing
- 88" x 108" piece of batting

*More than one fat quarter of the same print was included in the assortment.

CUTTING

All measurements include ¼" seam allowances.

From the beige print, cut:
- 7 strips, 6¼" x 42". Cut the strips into 41 squares, 6¼" x 6¼"; cut the squares in half diagonally twice to yield 164 triangles (2 extra).
- 4 strips, 3⅜" x 42". Cut the strips into 38 squares, 3⅜" x 3⅜"; cut the squares in half diagonally once to yield 76 triangles.
- 14 strips, 3" x 42". Cut the strips into:
  - 52 squares, 3" x 3"
  - 14 rectangles, 3" x 15½"
  - 28 rectangles, 3" x 5½"

From *each* of the 3 light tan tone-on-tone prints, cut:
- 2 strips, 6¼" x 21". Cut the strips into 4 squares, 6¼" x 6¼"; cut the squares in half diagonally twice to yield 16 triangles (48 total).
- 1 strip, 3⅜" x 21". Cut the strip into 5 squares, 3⅜" x 3⅜"; cut the squares in half diagonally once to yield 10 triangles (30 total).
- 3 squares, 3⅜" x 3⅜"; cut the squares in half diagonally once to yield 6 triangles (18 total)

From *each* of the 12 dark red, dark green, and dark blue prints, cut:
- 3 strips, 3⅜" x 21". Cut the strips into 12 squares, 3⅜" x 3⅜"; cut the squares in half diagonally once to yield 24 triangles (288 total).
- 1 square, 6¼" x 6¼"; cut the square in half diagonally twice to yield 4 triangles (48 total)

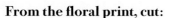

From the floral print, cut:

+ 3 strips, 11¼" x 42". Cut the strips into 7 squares, 11¼" x 11¼"; cut the squares in half diagonally twice to yield 28 triangles.
+ 1 strip, 5⅞" x 42". Cut the strip into 6 squares, 5⅞" x 5⅞"; cut the squares in half diagonally once to yield 12 triangles.

From the remainder of the floral print, selectively cut:

+ 12 squares, 5½" x 5½"

From *each* of 6 medium tan prints, cut:

+ 4 strips, 3⅜" x 21". Cut the strips into:
  - 16 squares, 3⅜" x 3⅜"; cut the squares in half diagonally once to yield 32 triangles (192 total)
  - 5 squares, 3" x 3" (30 total)
+ 1 strip, 3" x 21"; cut the strip into 6 squares, 3" x 3" (36 total)

From the remaining medium tan print, cut:

+ 3 strips, 3" x 21"; cut the strips into 14 squares, 3" x 3"

From *each* of 4 black prints, cut:

+ 5 strips, 3⅜" x 21". Cut the strips into 24 squares, 3⅜" x 3⅜"; cut the squares in half diagonally once to yield 48 triangles (192 total).

From *each* of the 4 remaining black prints, cut:

+ 1 square, 6¼" x 6¼"; cut the square in half diagonally twice to yield 4 triangles (16 total; 2 extra)
+ 7 squares, 3" x 3" (28 total)
+ 1 strip, 3⅜" x 21". Cut the strip into 5 squares, 3⅜" x 3⅜"; cut the squares in half diagonally once to yield 10 triangles (40 total; 4 extra).

From the navy tone-on-tone print, cut:

+ 3 strips, 11¼" x 42". Cut the strips into 8 squares, 11¼" x 11¼"; cut the squares in half diagonally twice to yield 32 triangles.
+ 1 strip, 5⅞" x 42". Cut the strip into 2 squares, 5⅞" x 5⅞"; cut the squares in half diagonally once to yield 4 triangles.

ASSEMBLY

1. Using the triangles cut from 3⅜" squares, sew a beige triangle to a light tan tone-on-tone triangle along their longest edges to form a half-square-triangle unit. Make 12 sets of four matching half-square triangles (48 total). Press the seam allowances toward the light tan triangles and trim the dog-ears.

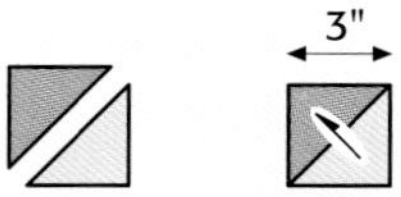

Make 48
in matching
sets of 4.

2. Sew two matching dark red triangles cut from 3⅜" squares to the short edges of a beige triangle cut from a 6¼" square to make a flying-geese unit. Make four sets of four matching flying-geese units (16 total). Repeat with the 3⅜" dark green and dark blue triangles. Press the seam allowances toward the dark triangles and trim the dog-ears.

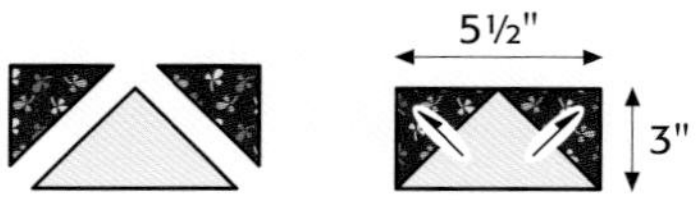

Make 16
in matching
sets of 4.

Make 16
in matching
sets of 4.

Make 16
in matching
sets of 4.

CLEVER TIP

Fabric Placement

When making the blocks, I matched the same light tan tone-on-tone and medium tan prints to each dark red, dark green, and dark blue print.

3. Arrange and sew the units from steps 1 and 2 and the floral print 5½" squares together into rows as shown. (The flying-geese units for each center block should be from the same dark fabric.) Press the seam allowances as indicated. Sew the rows together to make the Magic Cross blocks in the color combinations shown. Press the seam allowances as indicated.

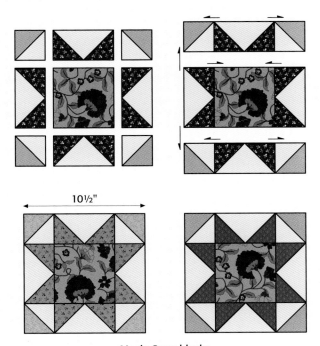

10½"

Magic Cross blocks.
Make 4 of each color combination.

4. Using the triangles cut from 3⅜" squares, refer to step 1 to make half-square-triangle units from the medium tan, dark red, dark green, and dark blue triangles as shown. Press the seam allowances toward the dark triangles and trim the dog-ears. Make four sets of eight matching half-square triangles (32 total) of each color combination.

3"

Make 32 in matching sets of 8.   Make 32 in matching sets of 8.   Make 32 in matching sets of 8.

5. Sew the remaining dark red, dark green, and dark blue triangles cut from 3⅜" squares to the light tan tone-on-tone triangles cut from 6¼" squares to make flying-geese units. Make four sets of four matching flying-geese units (16 total) of each color combination. Press the seam allowances toward the dark triangles and trim the dog-ears.

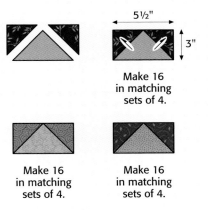

5½"   3"

Make 16 in matching sets of 4.

Make 16 in matching sets of 4.   Make 16 in matching sets of 4.

6. Sew the medium tan triangles cut from 3⅜" squares to the short edges of the dark red, dark green, and dark blue triangles cut from 6¼" squares to make flying-geese units. Make four sets of four flying-geese units (16 total) of each color combination. Press the seam allowances toward the medium tan triangles and trim the dog-ears.

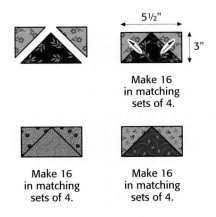

5½"   3"

Make 16 in matching sets of 4.

Make 16 in matching sets of 4.   Make 16 in matching sets of 4.

7. Sew the black triangles cut from 3⅜" squares to the short edges of the beige triangles cut from 6¼" squares. Press the seam allowances toward the black triangles and trim the dog-ears.

5½"   3"

Make 114.

8. Sew the units from steps 4–7 and the 3" squares cut from the beige and medium tan prints together as shown to form the block frames. (The dark red, dark green, and dark blue fabrics in each frame should match.) Press the seam allowances as indicated. Sew the frames to a like-colored Magic Cross block from step 3 to complete the framed blocks. Press the seam allowances as indicated. Make four blocks of each color and press the final seam allowances open.

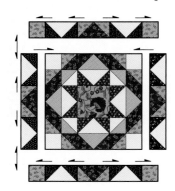

20½"

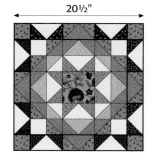 

Framed Magic Cross blocks.
Make 4 of each.

9. Referring to the quilt assembly diagram on page 29, arrange and sew the blocks into rows as shown. Press the seam allowances open. Sew the rows together. Press the seam allowances open.

10. Sew the remaining beige triangles cut from 3⅜" squares to the short edges of 14 black triangles cut from 6¼" squares. Press the seam allowances toward the beige triangles and trim the dog-ears.

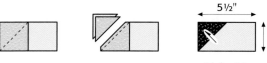

5½"

3"

Make 14.

11. With right sides together, place a black 3" square on the left-hand side of a beige 3" x 5½" rectangle. Draw a diagonal line through the square as shown and sew on the line. Leaving a ¼" seam allowance, trim away the excess fabric. Press the seam allowance toward the black print. Repeat to make 14 units.

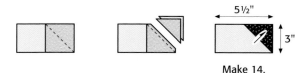

5½"

3"

Make 14.

12. Repeat step 12, sewing the remaining black squares to the right-hand side of the remaining beige 3" x 5½" rectangles.

5½"

3"

Make 14.

13. Sew the units from steps 10–12 and the remaining medium tan 3" squares together as shown to form the inner-border rows. Press the seam allowances as indicated.

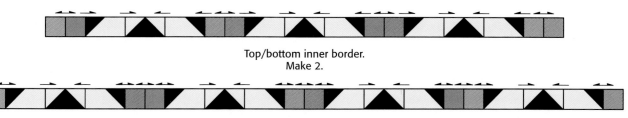

Top/bottom inner border.
Make 2.

Side inner border.
Make 2.

14. Referring to the quilt assembly diagram below right, sew the side inner borders to the quilt top as shown. Press the seam allowances toward the borders. Sew the top and bottom inner borders to the quilt top. Press the seam allowances toward the borders.

15. Sew the remaining units from step 7 to the remaining beige 3" squares and the beige 3" x 15½" rectangles to form the middle-border rows. Press the seam allowances toward the beige squares and rectangles.

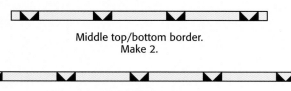

Middle top/bottom border.
Make 2.

Middle side border.
Make 2.

16. Referring to the quilt assembly diagram, sew the side middle borders to the quilt top as shown. Press the seam allowances toward the middle borders. Sew the top and bottom middle borders to the quilt top. Press the seam allowances toward the middle borders.

17. Using the triangles cut from 5⅞" squares, sew each navy triangle to a floral triangle along the longest edges to make half-square-triangle units. Press the seam allowances toward the navy triangles and trim the dog-ears.

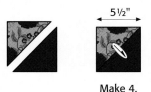

Make 4.

18. Sew the floral and navy triangles cut from 11¼" squares, the half-square-triangle units from step 17, and the remaining floral triangles cut from the 5⅞" squares together as shown to form the outer-border rows. Press the seam allowances toward the navy triangles and the half-square-triangle units.

Top/bottom outer border.
Make 2.

Top/bottom outer border.
Make 2.

19. Referring to the quilt assembly diagram, sew the side outer borders to the quilt top as shown. Press the seam allowances toward the outer borders. Sew the top and bottom outer borders to the quilt top. Press the seam allowances toward the outer borders.

20. Quilt as desired and bind. Refer to "Finishing Your Quilt" on page 17 for details if needed.

Quilt assembly

Baby Rails

Designed, sewn, and quilted by Susan Dissmore, 2005.

QUILT ESSENTIALS

FINISHED QUILT: 33" x 38" · FINISHED RAIL FENCE BLOCK: 5" x 5" · FAT QUARTERS REQUIRED: 5

Clever Fabric Choices: Five pastel fat quarters in colors of lavender, pink, yellow, green, and blue were sewn into Rail Fence blocks and then bordered with a coordinating baby print followed by a piano-key outer border using the same fabric combination.

MATERIALS

Yardages are based on 42"-wide fabric.

- 1 fat quarter *each* of green, blue, pink, yellow, and lavender fabric for Rail Fence blocks (5 total)
- ⅝ yard of multicolored print for inner border and outer-border corner squares
- ⅜ yard of fabric for binding
- 1⅜ yards of fabric for backing
- 41" x 46" piece of batting

CUTTING

All measurements include ¼" seam allowances.

From *each* of the green, blue, pink, yellow, and lavender prints, cut:
- 11 strips, 1½" x 21" (55 total)

From the multicolored print, cut:
- 1 strip, 4½" x 42"; cut the strip into 4 squares, 4½" x 4½"
- 4 strips, 3" x 42". Cut the strips into:
  - 2 rectangles, 3" x 20½"
  - 2 rectangles, 3" x 30½"

ASSEMBLY

1. Sew one strip of each of the five colors together as shown to make a strip set. Repeat to make a total of 11 strip sets, following the same order in each strip set. Press the seam allowances in one direction. From *each* of 10 of the strip sets, crosscut 2 Rail Fence blocks, 5½" x 5½", and 2 outer-border units, 4½" x 5½". From the remaining strip set, crosscut 2 outer-border units, 4½" x 5½". You'll have a total of 20 Rail Fence blocks and 22 outer-border units.

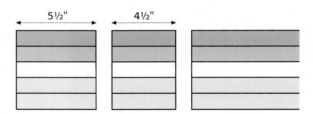

Make 11 strip sets.
Cut 20 squares, 5½" x 5½",
and 22 rectangles, 4½" x 5½".

2. Referring to the quilt assembly diagram on page 32, arrange and sew the Rail Fence blocks into rows as shown. Press the seam allowances as indicated. Sew the rows together to form the quilt center. Press the seam allowances in one direction.

3. Sew the multicolored 3" x 20½" rectangles to the top and bottom of the quilt center. Press the seam allowances toward the borders. Sew the multicolored 3" x 30½" rectangles to the sides of the quilt. Press the seam allowances toward the borders.

4. Sew the outer-border units from step 1 together end to end as shown. Press the seam allowances in one direction.

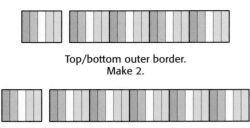

Top/bottom outer border.
Make 2.

Side outer border.
Make 2.

5. Referring to the quilt assembly diagram, sew the top and bottom outer-border strips to the quilt top as shown. Press the seam allowances toward the inner borders. Add a multicolored square to each end of the side outer-border strips and press the seam allowances toward the squares. Sew the side outer-border strips to the quilt top. Press the seam allowances toward the inner borders.

6. Quilt as desired and bind. Refer to "Finishing Your Quilt" on page 17 for details if needed.

Quilt assembly

Baby Rails Two!

Designed, sewn, and quilted by Susan Dissmore, 2004.

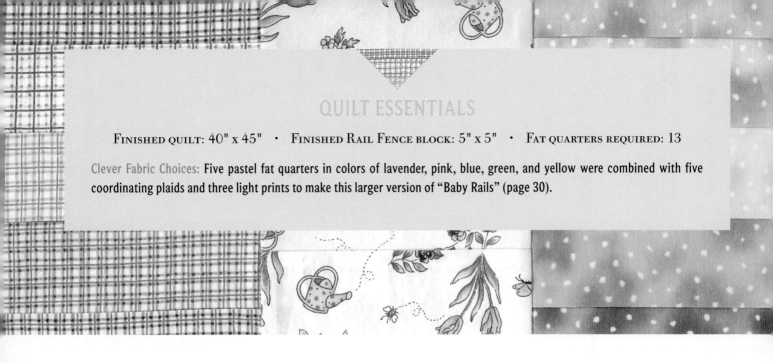

FINISHED QUILT: 40" x 45" · FINISHED RAIL FENCE BLOCK: 5" x 5" · FAT QUARTERS REQUIRED: 13

Clever Fabric Choices: Five pastel fat quarters in colors of lavender, pink, blue, green, and yellow were combined with five coordinating plaids and three light prints to make this larger version of "Baby Rails" (page 30).

MATERIALS

Yardages are based on 42"-wide fabric.

✦ 1 fat quarter *each* of green, blue, pink, yellow, and lavender tone-on-tone prints for center Rail Fence blocks (5 total)

✦ 1 fat quarter *each* of green, blue, pink, yellow, and lavender plaid prints for outer-border Rail Fence blocks (5 total)

✦ 3 fat quarters of assorted light prints for inner border

✦ ½ yard of fabric for binding

✦ 2¾ yards of fabric for backing

✦ 48" x 53" piece of batting

CUTTING

All measurements include ¼" seam allowances.

From *each* of the green, blue, pink, yellow, and lavender tone-on-tone prints, cut:

✦ 10 strips, 1½" x 21" (50 total)

From *each* of the 3 assorted light prints, cut:

✦ 3 strips, 3" x 21" (9 total)

From *each* of the green, blue, pink, yellow, and lavender plaids, cut:

✦ 10 strips, 1½" x 21" (50 total)

ASSEMBLY

1. Sew one strip of each of the five colors of tone-on-tone prints together as shown to make a strip set. Repeat to make a total of 10 strip sets, following the same order in each strip set. Press the seam allowances in one direction. Crosscut the strip sets into 30 Rail Fence blocks, 5½" x 5½". Repeat with the plaid strips.

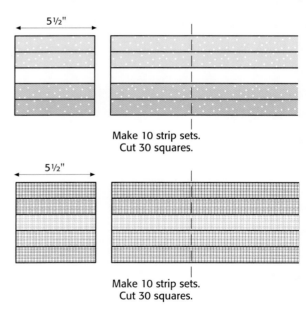

Make 10 strip sets.
Cut 30 squares.

Make 10 strip sets.
Cut 30 squares.

2. Referring to the quilt assembly diagram, arrange and sew the tone-on-tone Rail Fence blocks as shown. Press the seam allowances as indicated. Sew the rows together to form the quilt center. Press the seam allowances in one direction.

3. Sew one strip of each of the three colors of light prints together as shown to make a strip set. Repeat to make a total of three strip sets, following the same order in each strip set. Press the seam allowances in one direction. Crosscut the strip sets into 16 segments, 3" wide.

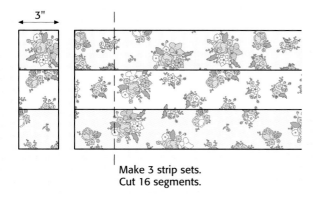

Make 3 strip sets.
Cut 16 segments.

4. Arrange and sew four segments from step 3 together end to end to make an inner-border strip. Repeat to make a total of four inner-border strips. Press the seam allowances in one direction.

Inner border.
Make 4.

5. Sew two of the inner-border strips from step 4 to the sides of the quilt top, re-pressing seam allowances where necessary so they oppose the block seam allowances. Press the seam allowances toward the inner border. Sew the remaining inner-border strips to the top and bottom of the quilt top in the same manner. Press the seam allowances toward the inner border.

6. Arrange and sew the plaid Rail Fence blocks together as shown for the outer border. Press the seam allowances in the opposite direction of the inner border. Sew the side outer borders to the quilt top. Press the seam allowances as desired. Sew the top and bottom outer borders to the quilt top. Press the seam allowances as desired.

Side outer border.
Make 2.

Top/bottom outer border.
Make 2.

7. Quilt as desired and bind. Refer to "Finishing Your Quilt" on page 17 for details if needed.

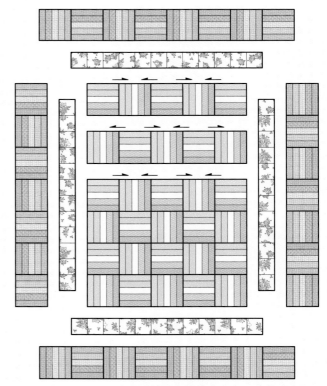

Quilt assembly

Briar Patch

Designed, sewn, and quilted by Susan Dissmore, 2005.

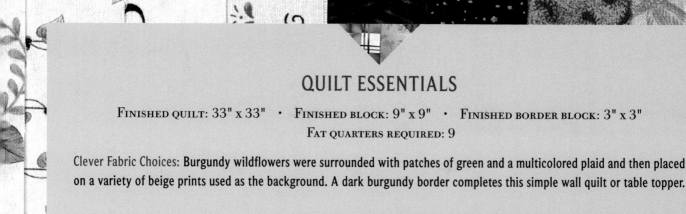

Clever Fabric Choices: Burgundy wildflowers were surrounded with patches of green and a multicolored plaid and then placed on a variety of beige prints used as the background. A dark burgundy border completes this simple wall quilt or table topper.

MATERIALS

Yardages are based on 42"-wide fabric.

- ✦ 3 fat quarters of assorted light beige prints for blocks and outer border (fabrics A, B, and C)
- ✦ 2 fat quarters of assorted burgundy prints for outer border
- ✦ 1 fat quarter of floral print for block centers
- ✦ 1 fat quarter of dark green print for blocks
- ✦ 1 fat quarter of medium green print for blocks
- ✦ 1 fat quarter of plaid for blocks
- ✦ ⅜ yard of fabric for binding
- ✦ 1¼ yards of fabric for backing
- ✦ 41" x 41" piece of batting

CUTTING

All measurements include ¼" seam allowances.

From 1 light beige print (A), cut:
- ✦ 3 strips, 4¼" x 21". Cut the strips into 12 squares, 4¼" x 4¼"; cut the squares in half diagonally twice to yield 48 triangles.

From the medium green print, cut:
- ✦ 3 strips, 4¼" x 21". Cut the strips into 9 squares, 4¼" x 4¼"; cut the squares in half diagonally twice to yield 36 triangles.

From the dark green print, cut:
- ✦ 4 strips, 3⅞" x 21". Cut the strips into 18 squares, 3⅞" x 3⅞"; cut the squares in half diagonally once to yield 36 triangles.

From *each* of the 2 remaining light beige prints (B and C), cut:
- ✦ 3 strips, 3⅞" x 21". Cut the strips into 15 squares, 3⅞" x 3⅞"; cut the squares in half diagonally once to yield 30 triangles (60 total).

From the plaid, cut:
- ✦ 4 strips, 3⅞" x 21". Cut the strips into 18 squares, 3⅞" x 3⅞"; cut the squares in half diagonally once to yield 36 triangles.

From the floral print, selectively cut:
- ✦ 9 squares, 3½" x 3½"

From 1 burgundy print, cut:
- ✦ 3 strips, 3⅞" x 21". Cut the strips into 12 squares, 3⅞" x 3⅞"; cut the squares in half diagonally once to yield 24 triangles.
- ✦ 4 squares, 3½" x 3½"

From the remaining burgundy print, cut:
- ✦ 2 strips, 3½" x 21"; cut the strips into 12 rectangles, 2" x 3½"
- ✦ 2 strips, 2⅜" x 21". Cut the strips into 12 squares, 2⅜" x 2⅜"; cut the squares in half diagonally once to yield 24 triangles.

ASSEMBLY

1. Using the triangles cut from 4¼" squares, sew a medium green triangle to a beige A triangle to form a larger triangle. Repeat to make 36. Press the seam allowances toward the green and trim the dog-ears. Reserve the remaining beige A triangles for the outer border.

Make 36.

2. Sew the dark green triangles cut from 3⅞" squares to each unit from step 1 to form a square. Press the seam allowances toward the dark green triangles and trim the dog-ears.

Make 36.

3. Using the triangles cut from 3⅞" squares, sew a plaid triangle to 18 beige B triangles and 18 beige C triangles. Press the seam allowances toward the plaid and trim the dog-ears. Reserve the remaining beige B and C triangles for the outer border.

Make 18.   Make 18.

4. Arrange and sew the floral print squares and the units from steps 1–3 together into rows. Press the seam allowances as indicated. Sew the rows together to form the block. Press the final seam allowances open.

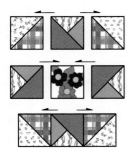   9½"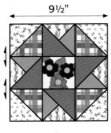

Make 9.

5. Referring to the quilt assembly diagram, arrange and sew the blocks into rows as shown. Press the seam allowances open. Sew the rows together. Press the seam allowances open.

6. Sew the burgundy triangles cut from 2⅜" squares to each short side of the remaining beige A triangles as shown. Press the seam allowances toward the burgundy and trim the dog-ears.

 3½" 2"

Make 12.

7. Sew the burgundy rectangles to the units from step 6 as shown. Press the seam allowances toward the rectangles.

 3½"

Make 12.

8. Using the triangles cut from 3⅞" squares, sew a burgundy triangle to each remaining beige B and C triangle along the longest edges. Press the seam allowances toward the burgundy triangles and trim the dog-ears.

 3½"

Make 12.   Make 12.

9. Sew the burgundy 3½" squares and the units from steps 7 and 8 together as shown to form the outer borders. Press the seam allowances so that they oppose the block seam allowances.

Side border.
Make 2.

Top/bottom border.
Make 2.

Size Option

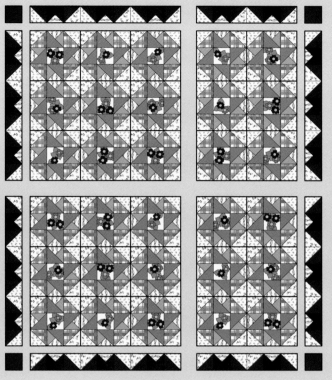

52" x 60"

Materials: Multiply each item in the "Briar Patch" materials list on page 37 by four to determine the amount of fat quarters required. For the floral, dark green, medium green, and plaid prints, consider choosing one *each* of four different colors to create a scrappy version of this quilt. Measure the finished quilt to determine the amount of yardage required for the backing and binding, and the size of the batting piece.

Assembly: Follow the assembly instructions on page 38 and below for the smaller version, increasing the amount of blocks as shown. If desired, add an additional outer border to further increase the size of the finished quilt. Just remember that adding a border will alter the amount of yardage required for the backing and binding, as well as the size of the batting piece.

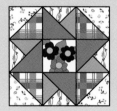

Make 30.

Make 22 of each.

10. Sew the side outer borders to the quilt top. Press the seam allowances open. Sew the top and bottom outer borders to the quilt top. Press the seam allowances open.

11. Quilt as desired and bind. Refer to "Finishing Your Quilt" on page 17 for details if needed.

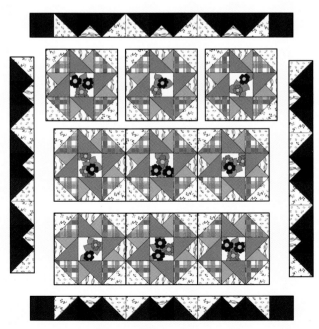

Quilt assembly

Brick and Mortar

Designed and sewn by Susan Dissmore; machine quilted by Eileen Peacher, 2005.

QUILT ESSENTIALS

FINISHED QUILT: 62" x 72" · FINISHED BLOCK: 10" x 10" · FAT QUARTERS REQUIRED: 26

Clever Fabric Choices: Deep shades of blue, green, rust, and red are stacked together with warm shades of beige in this quilt made from a prebundled collection of fat quarters. For a fun ending, use any extra fat quarters from the bundle to make the binding as I did.

MATERIALS

Yardages are based on 42"-wide fabric.

- 3 fat quarters *each* of assorted red, rust, green, and blue prints for blocks (12 total)
- 1 fat quarter *each* of brown, red, rust, gold, green, and blue tone-on-tone prints for outer border (6 total)
- 4 fat quarters of assorted tan prints for blocks
- 3 fat quarters of assorted tan tone-on-tone prints for inner border
- 1 fat quarter of dark blue print for outer-border corner squares
- ⅝ yard of fabric for binding
- 4 yards of fabric for backing
- 70" x 80" piece of batting

CUTTING

All measurements include ¼" seam allowances.

From *each* of the 4 assorted tan prints, cut:
- 5 strips, 2½" x 21" (20 total)

From *each* of 1 red, rust, green, and blue print, cut:
- 2 strips, 2½" x 21" (8 total)
- 2 strips, 4½" x 21" (8 total)

From *each* of the 2 remaining red, rust, green, and blue prints, cut:
- 1 strip, 6½" x 21"; cut the strip into 8 rectangles, 2½" x 6½" (64 total; 1 extra rectangle per color)
- 1 strip, 8½" x 21" (8 total)

From *each* of the 3 tan tone-on-tone prints, cut:
- 5 strips, 2½" x 21" (15 total)

From *each* of the assorted brown, red, rust, gold, green, and blue tone-on-tone prints, cut:
- 5 strips, 2½" x 21" (30 total)

From the dark blue print, cut:
- 1 strip, 4½" x 21"; cut the strip into 4 squares, 4½" x 4½"

ASSEMBLY

1. Sew 2½" x 21" strips of rust, tan, and green prints together as shown to make two strip sets. Press the seam allowances toward the rust and green strips. Crosscut the strip sets into 15 segments, 2½" wide. Repeat using 2½" x 21" strips of blue, tan, and red prints.

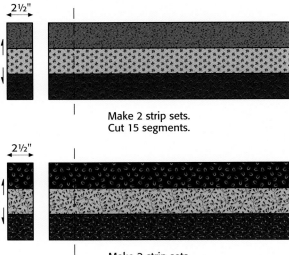

Make 2 strip sets.
Cut 15 segments.

Make 2 strip sets.
Cut 15 segments.

2. Sew a tan print 2½" x 21" strip to one long edge of the 4½" x 21" strips cut from the red, rust, green, and blue prints to make strip sets. Press the seam allowances toward the dark fabrics. Crosscut each pair of strip sets into 15 segments, 2½" wide.

3. Repeat step 2 using the remaining tan print 2½" x 21" strips and the 8½" x 21" strips cut from the red, rust, green, and blue prints.

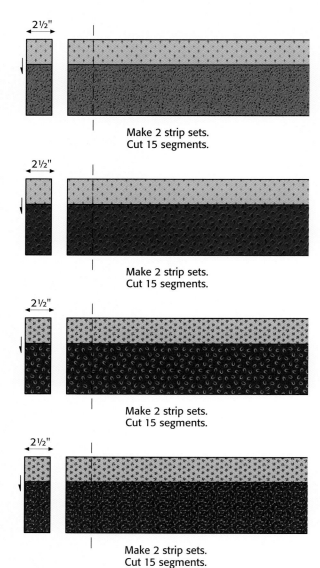

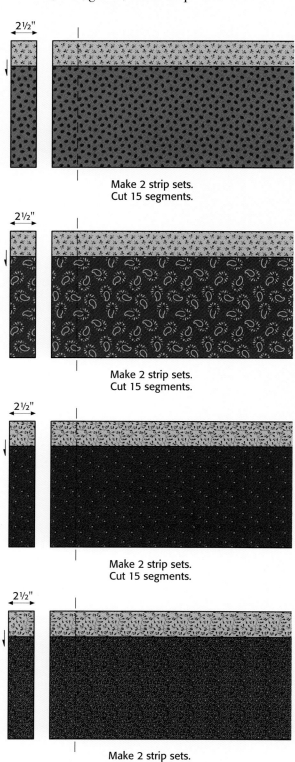

4. Sew the 2½" x 6½" rectangles of red, rust, green, and blue prints together with the segments from steps 1–3 as shown to make blocks A and B. Press the seam allowances as indicated.

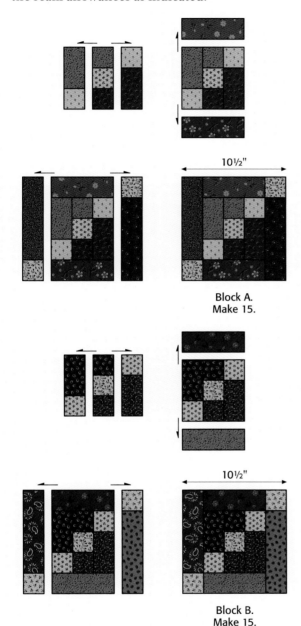

Block A.
Make 15.

Block B.
Make 15.

5. Referring to the quilt assembly diagram on page 44, arrange and sew the blocks into rows as shown, alternating the placement of blocks A and B in each row and from row to row. Press the seam allowances in opposite directions from row to row. Sew the rows together. Press the seam allowances in one direction.

6. Sew one 2½" x 21" strip of each of the three tan tone-on-tone prints together to make a strip set. Repeat to make a total of five strip sets, following the same order in each strip set. Press the seam allowances in one direction. Crosscut the strip sets into 38 segments, 2½" wide.

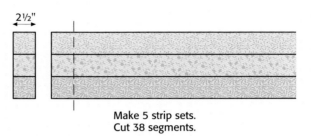

2½"

Make 5 strip sets.
Cut 38 segments.

7. To make the top and bottom inner borders, sew 9 of the segments from step 6 together end to end to form one long strip. Repeat to make two strips. Press the seam allowances in one direction. To make the side inner borders, sew 10 segments from step 6 together in the same manner. Make two. Press the seam allowances in one direction.

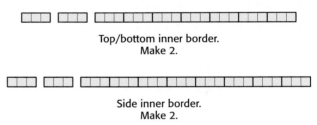

Top/bottom inner border.
Make 2.

Side inner border.
Make 2.

8. Referring to the quilt assembly diagram, sew the top and bottom inner borders to the quilt. Press the seam allowances toward the inner border. Sew the side inner borders to the quilt. Press the seam allowances toward the inner border.

9. Sew one 2½" x 21" strip each of brown, blue, green, gold, rust, and red tone-on-tone prints together into a strip set. Repeat to make a total of five strip sets, following the same order in each strip set. Press the seam allowances in one direction. Crosscut the strip sets into 20 segments, 4½" wide.

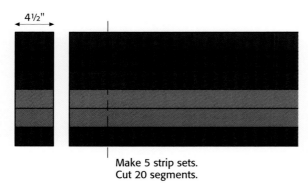

4½"

Make 5 strip sets.
Cut 20 segments.

10. To make the outer borders, sew five segments from step 9 together end to end to form one long strip. Repeat to make a total of four strips. Press the seam allowances in one direction. Remove three rectangles from the right-hand end of two outer-border strips to make the top and bottom outer borders. Sew the removed segments to the left-hand side of the remaining two outer-border strips. Remove one rectangle from the opposite end of each strip to make the side outer borders.

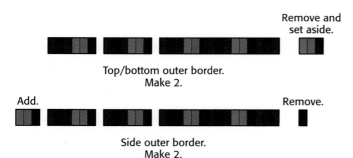

Remove and
set aside.

Top/bottom outer border.
Make 2.

Add.   Remove.

Side outer border.
Make 2.

11. Sew the side outer borders to the quilt top, re-pressing seam allowances where necessary so they oppose the inner-border seams. Press the seam allowances toward the outer borders. Sew a dark blue square to each end of the top and bottom outer-border strips. Sew the borders to the quilt top, re-pressing seam allowances where necessary. Press the seam allowances toward the outer borders.

12. Quilt as desired and bind. Refer to "Finishing Your Quilt" on page 17 for details if needed.

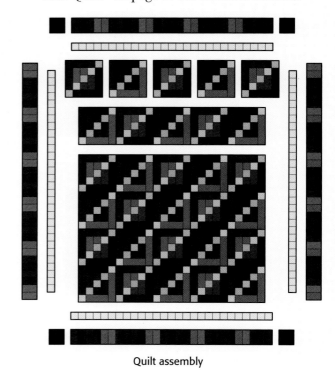

Quilt assembly

Charmed, I'm Sure

Designed and sewn by Susan Dissmore; machine quilted by Eileen Peacher, 2004.

QUILT ESSENTIALS

FINISHED QUILT: 66" x 78" · FINISHED STAR BLOCK: 12" x 12" · FINISHED BORDER SIDE BLOCK: 9" x 12"
FINISHED BORDER CORNER BLOCK: 9" x 9" · FAT QUARTERS REQUIRED: 37

Clever Fabric Choices: Follow the color-wheel concept discussed in "Choosing Fat Quarters" on page 9 to select seven dark hand-dyed fat quarters. Then choose seven fat quarters each of medium-value prints and medium-dark value prints. Once you've done that, all that's left are the light and black pieces—the easy ones!

MATERIALS

Yardages are based on 42"-wide fabric.

- 9 fat quarters of assorted light prints for blocks and outer border*
- 7 fat quarters of assorted black prints for outer border*
- 1 fat quarter *each* of dark prints in green, blue, red, brown, purple, gold, and gray for blocks and outer border (7 total)
- 1 fat quarter *each* of medium-dark prints in green, blue, red, brown, purple, gold, and gray for blocks and outer border (7 total)
- 1 fat quarter *each* of medium prints in green, blue, red, brown, purple, gold, and gray for blocks and outer border (7 total)
- ¾ yard of fabric for binding
- 5 yards of fabric for backing
- 74" x 86" piece of batting

*More than one fat quarter of the same print was included in the assortment.

CUTTING

All measurements include ¼" seam allowances.

From *each* of the dark and medium green, blue, red, brown, and purple prints, cut:

- 3 strips, 3⅞" x 21". Cut the strips into 12 squares, 3⅞" x 3⅞"; cut the squares in half diagonally once to yield 24 triangles (240 total).
- 1 strip, 4¼" x 21". Cut the strip into 4 squares, 4¼" x 4¼"; cut the squares in half diagonally twice to yield 16 triangles (160 total).

From *each* of the medium-dark green, blue, red, brown, purple, and gray prints, cut:

- 2 strips, 3⅞" x 21". Cut the strips into 9 squares, 3⅞" x 3⅞"; cut the squares in half diagonally once to yield 18 triangles (108 total; 1 extra of green, blue, brown, and gray).
- 1 strip, 4¼" x 21". Cut the strip into 4 squares, 4¼" x 4¼"; cut the squares in half diagonally twice to yield 16 triangles (96 total).

From the dark gray print, cut:

- 3 strips, 3⅞" x 21". Cut the strips into 12 squares, 3⅞" x 3⅞"; cut the squares in half diagonally once to yield 24 triangles.

From the medium gray print, cut:

- 3 strips, 3⅞" x 21". Cut the strips into 12 squares, 3⅞" x 3⅞"; cut the squares in half diagonally once to yield 24 triangles.
- 1 strip, 4¼" x 21". Cut the strip into 4 squares, 4¼" x 4¼"; cut the squares in half diagonally twice to yield 16 triangles.

From *each* of the dark, medium-dark, and medium gold prints, cut:

- 2 strips, 3⅞" x 21". Cut the strips into 8 squares, 3⅞" x 3⅞"; cut the squares in half diagonally once to yield 16 triangles (48 total).
- 1 strip, 4¼" x 21". Cut the strip into 4 squares, 4¼" x 4¼"; cut the squares in half diagonally twice to yield 16 triangles (48 total).

From *each* of 6 assorted light prints, cut:

- 3 squares, 7¼" x 7¼"; cut the squares in half diagonally twice to yield 12 triangles for blocks (72 total).
- 6 squares, 3⅞" x 3⅞"; cut the squares in half diagonally once to yield 12 triangles (72 total).

From 1 of the remaining light prints, cut:

- 1 strip, 7¼" x 21". Cut the strip into 2 squares, 7¼" x 7¼"; cut the squares in half diagonally twice to yield 8 triangles for blocks.
- 1 strip, 3⅞" x 21". Cut the strip into 4 squares, 3⅞" x 3⅞"; cut the squares in half diagonally once to yield 8 triangles.

From *each* of the 2 remaining light prints, cut:

- 2 strips, 7¼" x 21". Cut the strips into 3 squares, 7¼" x 7¼"; cut the squares in half diagonally twice to yield 12 triangles for border (24 total; 3 extra per print).

From *each* of 4 black prints, cut:

- 1 square, 7¼" x 7¼"; cut the square in half diagonally twice to yield 4 triangles (16 total)
- 4 rectangles, 3½" x 12½" (16 total)

From 1 black print, cut:

- 2 strips, 3⅞" x 21". Cut the strips into 10 squares, 3⅞" x 3⅞"; cut the squares in half diagonally once to yield 20 triangles.
- 1 square, 7¼" x 7¼"; cut the square in half diagonally twice to yield 4 triangles (2 extra)
- 2 rectangles, 3½" x 12½"

From 1 black print, cut:

- 3 strips, 3⅞" x 21". Cut the strips into 14 squares, 3⅞" x 3⅞"; cut the squares in half diagonally once to yield 28 triangles.

From 1 black print, cut:

- 4 strips, 3½" x 21". Cut the strips into:
  - 4 rectangles, 3½" x 6½"
  - 4 rectangles, 3½" x 9½"

ASSEMBLY

1. Using the dark triangles cut from 3⅞" squares, sew two matching triangles to each short side of the light triangles (designated for blocks) cut from 7¼" squares as shown. Make the amount indicated for each color. Press the seam allowances toward the dark triangles and trim the dog-ears.

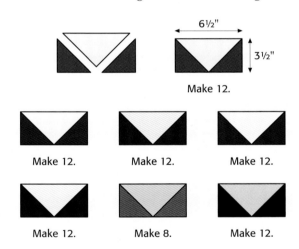

Make 12.

Make 12.   Make 12.   Make 12.

Make 12.   Make 8.   Make 12.

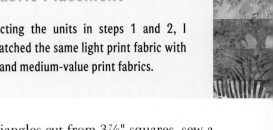

CLEVER TIP

Fabric Placement

When constructing the units in steps 1 and 2, I consistently matched the same light print fabric with the same dark and medium-value print fabrics.

2. Using the triangles cut from 3⅞" squares, sew a medium triangle to a light triangle along their longest edges to make a half-square-triangle unit. Make the amount indicated for each color. Press

the seam allowances toward the medium triangles and trim the dog-ears.

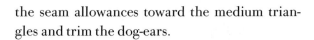

Make 12.

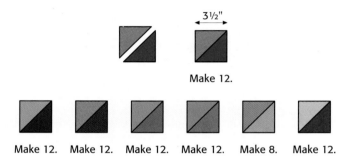

Make 12.   Make 12.   Make 12.   Make 12.   Make 8.   Make 12.

3. Repeat step 2 using the medium and medium-dark triangles. Press the seam allowances toward the medium-dark triangles and trim the dog-ears.

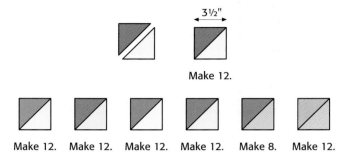

Make 12.

Make 12.   Make 12.   Make 12.   Make 12.   Make 8.   Make 12.

4. Sew the units from step 3 together as shown to make pinwheel units. Press the seam allowances as indicated. Press the final seam allowance open.

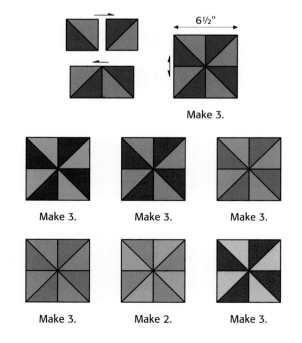

Make 3.

Make 3.   Make 3.   Make 3.

Make 3.   Make 2.   Make 3.

5. Sew the units from steps 1, 2, and 4 together in rows as shown to make the Star blocks. Press the seam allowances as indicated. Make a total of 20 blocks in the color combinations shown.

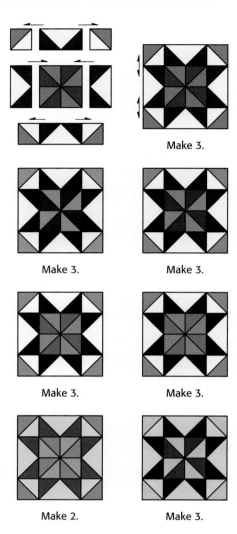

Make 3.

Make 3.   Make 3.

Make 3.   Make 3.

Make 2.   Make 3.

6. Using the triangles cut from medium and medium-dark green, blue, red, brown, purple, and gold 4¼" squares, sew the triangles together as shown to make larger triangles. Make eight of each color combination. Press the seam allowances toward the darker fabric and trim the dog-ears.

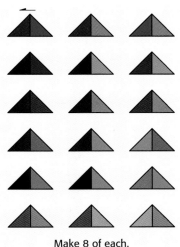

Make 8 of each.

7. Referring to the color combinations for the border blocks shown in the illustration at right, arrange the triangle units from step 6, the triangles cut from black and light 7¼" squares, and the triangles cut from black and medium-dark 3⅞" squares into two rows as shown. Sew the pieces in each row together. Press the seam allowances as indicated. Sew the rows together. Press the seam allowances open and trim the dog-ears. Add a black 3½" x 12½" rectangle to the top of each unit. Press the seam allowances toward the rectangles. Make one of each color combination.

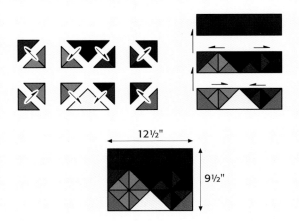

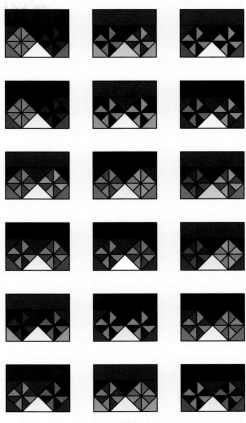

Border blocks.
Make 1 of each.

8. As described in step 6, sew the medium and medium-dark gray triangles cut from 4¼" squares together to make larger triangles.

Make 16.

9. Sew the gray triangles from step 8 to the remaining black and medium-dark gray, blue, green, and brown triangles cut from 3⅞" squares as shown. Don't press the seam allowances at this time.

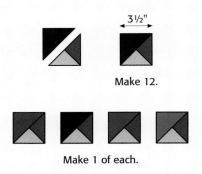

3½"

Make 12.

Make 1 of each.

10. Arrange and sew the units from step 9 together as shown. Press the seam allowances as indicated. Press the final seam allowance open.

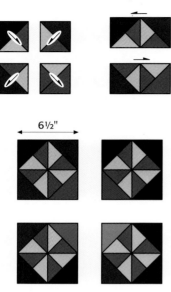

6½"

Make 1 of each.

11. Sew a black 3½" x 6½" rectangle to one side of each unit from step 10 as shown. Press the seam allowances toward the rectangles. Sew a black 3½" x 9½" rectangle to the top of each unit to complete the border corner blocks. Press the seam allowances toward the rectangles.

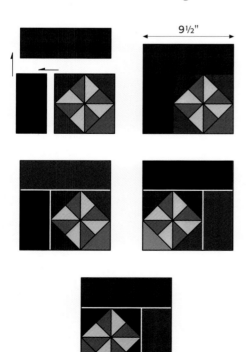

9½"

Border corner blocks.
Make 1 of each.

12. Referring to the quilt assembly diagram, arrange and sew the Star blocks, the border blocks, and the border corner blocks into rows as shown. Press the seam allowances open. Sew the rows together to form the quilt top. Press the seam allowances open.

13. Quilt as desired and bind. Refer to "Finishing Your Quilt" on page 17 for details if needed.

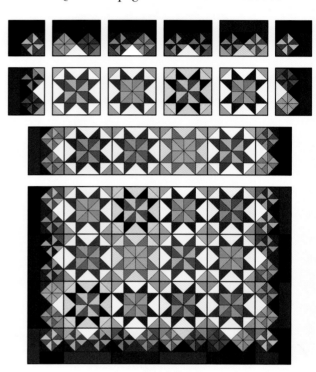

Quilt assembly

Farmer's Market

Designed and sewn by Susan Dissmore; machine quilted by Sue Gantt, 2005.

FINISHED QUILT: 66" x 78" • FINISHED HALF-SQUARE TRIANGLE BLOCKS: 6" x 6" and 3" x 3"
FAT QUARTERS REQUIRED: 38

Clever Fabric Choices: The weekend farmer's market is open for business with this quilt that started with a prebundled collection of fruit and vegetable prints. A variety of prints from several color families will be needed to fill up your "produce stand." Pick darker tone-on-tone prints for the inner and outer borders.

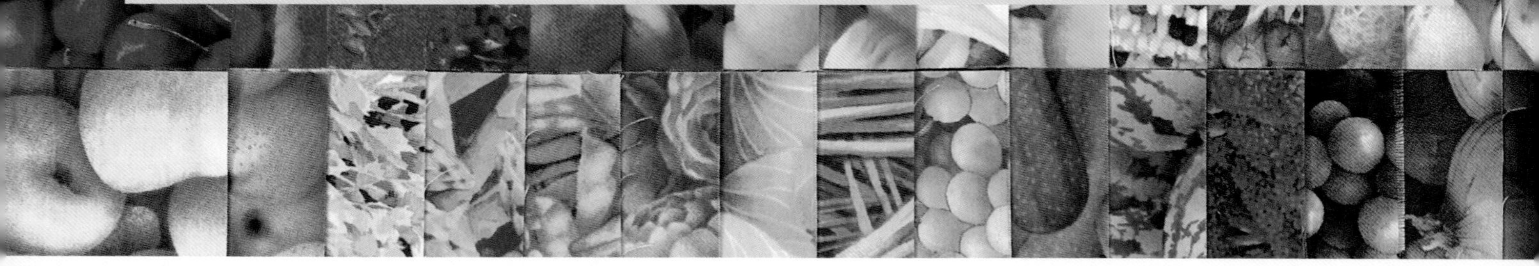

MATERIALS

Yardages are based on 42"-wide fabric.

- 12 fat quarters of assorted green prints for blocks and middle border
- 8 fat quarters of assorted red and orange prints for blocks and middle border
- 4 fat quarters of assorted yellow prints for blocks and middle border
- 4 fat quarters of assorted medium purple tone-on-tone prints for inner border
- 4 fat quarters of assorted dark purple tone-on-tone prints for outer border
- 3 fat quarters of assorted purple prints for blocks
- 3 fat quarters of assorted light brown prints for blocks
- ⅝ yard of fabric for binding
- 4¼ yards of fabric for backing
- 74" x 86" piece of batting

CUTTING

All measurements include ¼" seam allowances.

From *each* of 8 assorted green prints, cut:

- 2 squares, 6⅞" x 6⅞"; cut the squares in half diagonally once to yield 4 triangles (32 total)
- 4 squares, 3⅞" x 3⅞"; cut the squares in half diagonally once to yield 8 triangles (64 total)

From *each* of the 4 remaining assorted green prints, cut:

- 3 squares, 6⅞" x 6⅞"; cut the squares in half diagonally once to yield 6 triangles (24 total)
- 3 squares, 3⅞" x 3⅞"; cut the squares in half diagonally once to yield 6 triangles (24 total; 4 extra)

From *each* of 4 assorted red and orange prints, cut:

- 2 squares, 6⅞" x 6⅞"; cut the squares in half diagonally once to yield 4 triangles (16 total)
- 4 squares, 3⅞" x 3⅞"; cut the squares in half diagonally once to yield 8 triangles (32 total)

From *each* of the 4 remaining assorted red and orange prints, cut:

- 3 squares, 6⅞" x 6⅞"; cut the squares in half diagonally once to yield 6 triangles (24 total)
- 3 squares, 3⅞" x 3⅞"; cut the squares in half diagonally once to yield 6 triangles (24 total; 4 extra)

From *each* of the 4 assorted yellow prints, cut:

- 2 squares, 6⅞" x 6⅞"; cut the squares in half diagonally once to yield 4 triangles (16 total)
- 4 squares, 3⅞" x 3⅞"; cut the squares in half diagonally once to yield 8 triangles (32 total)

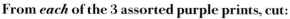

From *each* of the 3 assorted purple prints, cut:

✦ 4 squares, 6⅞" x 6⅞"; cut the squares in half diagonally once to yield 8 triangles (24 total)

From *each* of the 3 assorted light brown prints, cut:

✦ 4 squares, 6⅞" x 6⅞"; cut the squares in half diagonally once to yield 8 triangles (24 total)

From *each* of the 4 medium purple tone-on-tone prints, cut:

✦ 4 strips, 3½" x 21" (16 total)

From *each* of the 4 dark purple tone-on-tone prints, cut:

✦ 2 strips, 6½" x 21"; cut the strips into 10 rectangles, 3½" x 6½" (40 total)

✦ 1 strip, 3½" x 21"; cut the strip into:
  • 1 rectangle, 3½" x 6½" (4 total)
  • 1 square, 3½" x 3½" (4 total)

ASSEMBLY

1. Sew the triangles cut from 6⅞" squares together along their longest edges to form large Half-Square Triangle blocks in the color combinations shown. Press the seam allowances toward the darkest fabric in each block and trim the dog-ears.

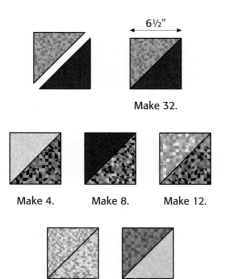

Make 32.

Make 4.   Make 8.   Make 12.

Make 12.   Make 12.

2. Referring to the quilt assembly diagram on page 54, arrange and sew the blocks from step 1 into rows as shown. Press the seam allowances in opposite directions from row to row. Sew the rows together. Press the seam allowances toward the top of the quilt.

3. Sew one 3½" x 21" strip of each of the assorted medium purple prints together to make a strip set. Repeat to make a total of four strip sets, following the same order. Press the seam allowances in one direction. Crosscut the strip sets into 19 segments, 3½" wide.

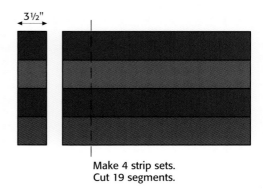

3½"

Make 4 strip sets.
Cut 19 segments.

4. Remove the center seam from one segment from step 3 to make two segments of two squares each as shown.

5. To make the top and bottom inner borders, sew four segments from step 3 together end to end as shown. Repeat to make two. To make the side inner borders, sew five segments from step 3 and one segment from step 4 together as shown. Repeat to make two. Press the seam allowances in one direction.

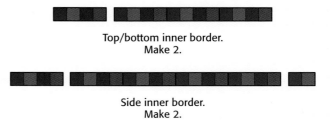

Top/bottom inner border.
Make 2.

Side inner border.
Make 2.

Note: The strips can be flipped when sewn to the quilt, so pressing in just one direction is fine for all border units.

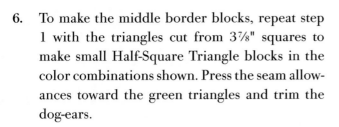

6. To make the middle border blocks, repeat step 1 with the triangles cut from 3⅞" squares to make small Half-Square Triangle blocks in the color combinations shown. Press the seam allowances toward the green triangles and trim the dog-ears.

3½"

Make 52.   Make 32.

7. To make the top and bottom middle borders, sew 18 blocks from step 6 together end to end as shown. Repeat to make two. To make the side middle borders, sew 24 blocks from step 6 together end to end as shown. Repeat to make two. Press the seam allowances in the opposite direction of the inner border.

Top/bottom middle border.
Make 2.

Side middle border.
Make 2.

8. To make the top and bottom outer borders, sew 10 of the dark purple 3½" x 6½" rectangles together end to end as shown. Repeat to make two. To make the side outer borders, sew 12 of the dark purple rectangles together end to end as shown. Add a dark purple square to each end of the strip. Repeat to make two. Press the seam allowances in the opposite direction of the middle border.

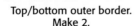

Top/bottom outer border.
Make 2.

Side outer border.
Make 2.

9. Referring to the quilt assembly diagram, position and sew the top and bottom inner borders to the quilt top, making sure that the border seam allowances are pressed in the opposite direction of the block seam allowances. Press the seam allowances toward the inner border. Repeat with the side inner borders. Press the seam allowances toward the inner border.

10. Repeat step 9 with the middle and outer borders, making sure that the seam allowances are pressed in the opposite direction of the previously added border. Press the seam allowances toward the newly added border.

Quilt assembly

11. Quilt as desired and bind. Refer to "Finishing Your Quilt" on page 17 for details if needed.

Finally Fall

Designed and sewn by Susan Dissmore; machine quilted by Eileen Peacher, 2004.

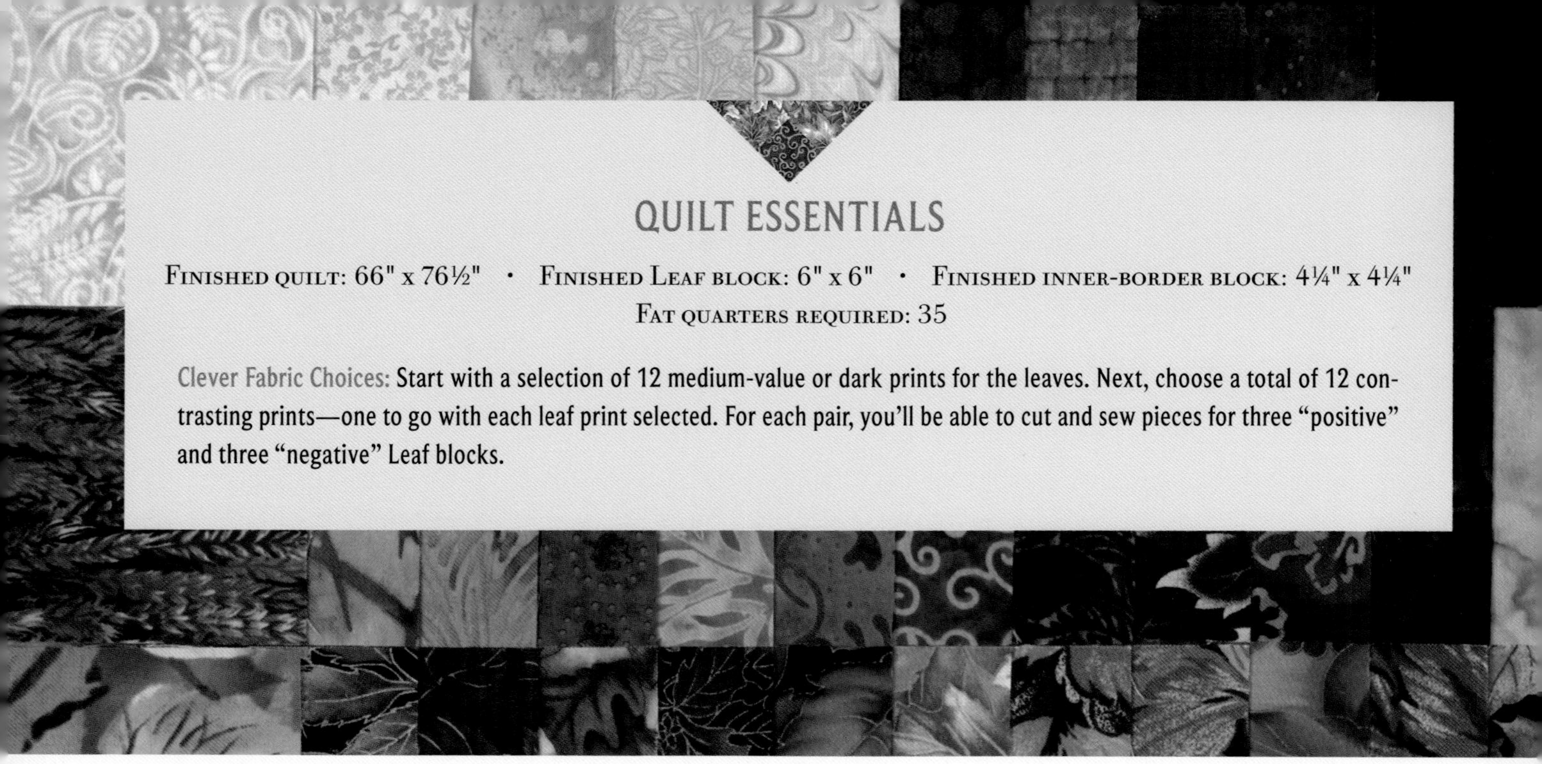

QUILT ESSENTIALS

FINISHED QUILT: 66" x 76½" · FINISHED LEAF BLOCK: 6" x 6" · FINISHED INNER-BORDER BLOCK: 4¼" x 4¼"

FAT QUARTERS REQUIRED: 35

Clever Fabric Choices: Start with a selection of 12 medium-value or dark prints for the leaves. Next, choose a total of 12 contrasting prints—one to go with each leaf print selected. For each pair, you'll be able to cut and sew pieces for three "positive" and three "negative" Leaf blocks.

MATERIALS

Yardages are based on 42"-wide fabric.

- 12 fat quarters of assorted leaf prints for Leaf blocks and inner border
- 12 fat quarters of assorted contrasting prints for Leaf blocks and inner border
- 1 fat quarter *each* of dark blue, dark green, dark rust, dark purple, dark gold, and dark brown tone-on-tone prints for outer border (6 total)
- 5 fat quarters of assorted beige prints for setting triangles and inner border
- ¾ yard of fabric for binding
- 4¾ yards of fabric for backing
- 76" x 85" piece of batting

CUTTING

All measurements include ¼" seam allowances.

From *each* of 10 leaf prints, cut:
- 2 strips, 2⅞" x 21". Cut the strips into 12 squares, 2⅞" x 2⅞"; cut the squares in half diagonally once to yield 24 triangles (240 total).
- 1 strip, 2½" x 21". Cut the strip into:
  - 3 rectangles, 2½" x 4½" (30 total)
  - 2 squares, 2½" x 2½" (20 total)

- 1 strip, 2½" x 21". Cut the strip into 1 square, 2½" x 2½" (10 total). Reserve the remainder of the strip.
- 2 squares, 5½" x 5½"; cut the squares in half diagonally twice to yield 8 triangles (80 total)

From *each* of the 2 remaining leaf prints, cut:
- 2 strips, 2⅞" x 21". Cut the strips into 12 squares, 2⅞" x 2⅞"; cut the squares in half diagonally once to yield 24 triangles (48 total).
- 1 strip, 2½" x 21". Cut the strip into:
  - 3 rectangles, 2½" x 4½" (6 total)
  - 2 squares, 2½" x 2½" (4 total)
- 1 strip, 2½" x 21". Cut the strip into 1 square, 2½" x 2½" (2 total). Reserve the remainder of the strip.
- 3 squares, 5½" x 5½"; cut the squares in half diagonally twice to yield 12 triangles (24 total)

From *each* of 10 contrasting prints, cut:
- 2 strips, 2⅞" x 21". Cut the strips into 12 squares, 2⅞" x 2⅞"; cut the squares in half diagonally once to yield 24 triangles (240 total).
- 1 strip, 2½" x 21". Cut the strip into:
  - 3 rectangles, 2½" x 4½" (30 total)
  - 2 squares, 2½" x 2½" (20 total)
- 1 strip, 2½" x 21". Cut the strip into 1 square, 2½" x 2½" (10 total). Reserve the remainder of the strip.
- 1 square, 5½" x 5½"; cut the square in half diagonally twice to yield 4 triangles (40 total)

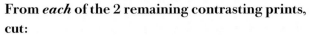

From *each* of the 2 remaining contrasting prints, cut:

✦ 2 strips, 2⅞" x 21". Cut the strips into 12 squares, 2⅞" x 2⅞"; cut the squares in half diagonally once to yield 24 triangles (48 total).

✦ 1 strip, 2½" x 21". Cut the strip into:
  - 3 rectangles, 2½" x 4½" (6 total)
  - 2 squares, 2½" x 2½" (4 total)

✦ 1 strip, 2½" x 21". Cut the strip into 1 square, 2½" x 2½" (2 total). Reserve the remainder of the strip.

✦ 2 squares, 5½" x 5½"; cut the squares in half diagonally twice to yield 8 triangles (16 total; 2 extra from each print)

✦ 1 square, 5⅛" x 5⅛"; cut the square in half diagonally once to yield 2 triangles (4 total)

From *each* of 3 beige prints, cut:

✦ 1 strip, 9¾" x 21". Cut the strip into 2 squares, 9¾" x 9¾"; cut the squares in half diagonally twice to yield 8 triangles (24 total; 2 extra).

✦ 1 strip, 5½" x 21". Cut the strip into 3 squares, 5½" x 5½"; cut the squares in half diagonally twice to yield 12 triangles (36 total).

From *each* of the 2 remaining beige prints, cut:

✦ 2 squares, 5⅛" x 5⅛"; cut the square in half diagonally once to yield 4 triangles (8 total)

✦ 1 strip, 5½" x 21". Cut the strip into 2 squares, 5½" x 5½"; cut the squares in half diagonally twice to yield 8 triangles (16 total).

From *each* of the 6 tone-on-tone prints, cut:

✦ 3 strips, 4¾" x 21" (18 total)

ASSEMBLY

1. Using the triangles cut from 2⅞" squares, match and sew each triangle from one leaf print to the same contrasting-print triangle along the longest edges to form half-square-triangle units. Press the seam allowances toward the darker fabric and trim the dog-ears. Make 24. Repeat with the remaining 11 color combinations.

Make 24 each of
12 color combinations
(288 total).

2. Pairing the same leaf and contrasting prints used in step 1, sew the reserved 2½"-wide strips together into strip sets. Make 1 strip set in each color combination (12 total). Press the seam allowances toward the darker fabric. Crosscut each strip set into six segments, 2½" wide.

Make 1 strip set of each color combination (12 total).
Cut 6 segments from each strip set (72 total).

3. Sew the 2½" x 4½" rectangles of leaf and contrasting prints to the corresponding units from step 2. Press the seam allowances toward the rectangles.

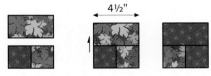

Make 3 of each
color combination
(72 total).

4. Arrange and sew the corresponding 2½" squares of leaf and contrasting prints together along with the units from steps 1 and 3 as shown to make the Leaf blocks. Make three "positive" and three "negative" blocks for each color combination. Press the seam allowances as indicated.

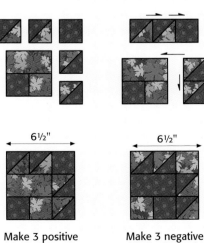

Make 3 positive
blocks for each
color combination
(36 total).

Make 3 negative
blocks for each
color combination
(36 total).

5. Using the triangles cut from 5½" squares, sew a leaf-print triangle to a contrasting-print triangle to make a larger triangle. Make 52. Repeat using a leaf-print triangle and a beige triangle. Make 52. Press the seam allowances toward the leaf print.

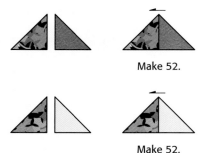

Make 52.

Make 52.

6. Sew the units from step 5 together as shown to make quarter-square-triangle units matching the same leaf print. Press the seam allowances toward the darker combination of triangles and trim the dog-ears.

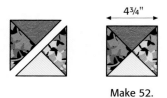

Make 52.

7. Using the triangles cut from 5⅛" squares, sew each contrasting-print triangle to a beige triangle along their longest edges to form half-square-triangle units. Press the seam allowances toward the contrasting-print triangles and trim the dog-ears.

Make 2.   Make 2.

8. Randomly sew 12 units from step 6 together end to end as shown. Add a unit from step 7 to each end to form the top and bottom inner borders. Randomly sew 14 units from step 6 together end to end as shown to form the side inner borders. Press the seam allowances in one direction.

Top/bottom inner border.
Make 2.

Side inner border.
Make 2.

9. Sew the 4¾"-wide strips cut from the tone-on-tone prints together into three strip sets as shown. Press the seam allowances in one direction. Crosscut the strip sets into 11 segments, 4¾" wide.

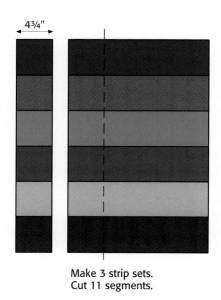

Make 3 strip sets.
Cut 11 segments.

10. Sew the segments from step 9 together end to end to form one long strip. Don't press the seam allowances at this time. Count 16 squares from one end of the strip and unsew the seam. Repeat to make four outer-border strips of 16 squares each.

11. Referring to the quilt assembly diagram, sew the blocks and beige setting triangles together into rows. Press the seam allowances in opposite directions from row to row. Sew the rows together. Press the seam allowances open.

CLEVER TIP

Consider using a design wall to determine the placement of the Leaf blocks in the quilt. I like to arrange them randomly and then walk away from them for a day or so. When I return, misplacements tend to stand out where I hadn't seen them before.

12. Referring to the quilt assembly diagram, sew the side inner borders from step 8 to the quilt top as shown. Press the seam allowances toward the quilt top. Repeat with the top and bottom inner borders.

13. Place an outer-border strip from step 10 along each side of the quilt top. Press the seam allowances in the opposite direction of the inner-border seam allowances. Sew the side outer borders to the quilt top. Press the seam allowances toward the outer borders. Repeat with the top and bottom outer borders.

14. Quilt as desired and bind. Refer to "Finishing Your Quilt" on page 17 for details if needed.

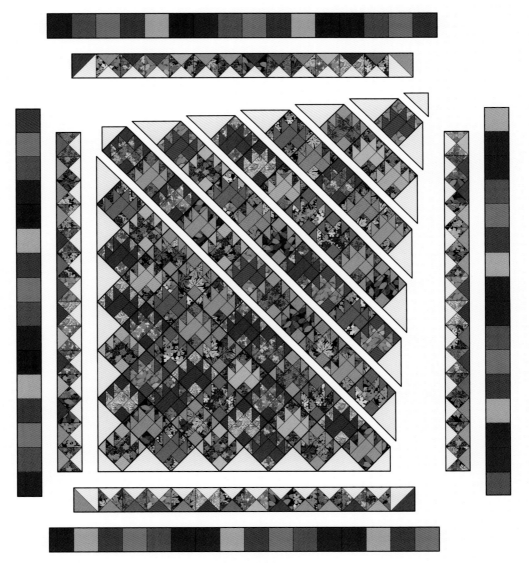

Quilt assembly

Floral Foursome

Designed and sewn by Susan Dissmore; machine quilted by Eileen Peacher, 2003.

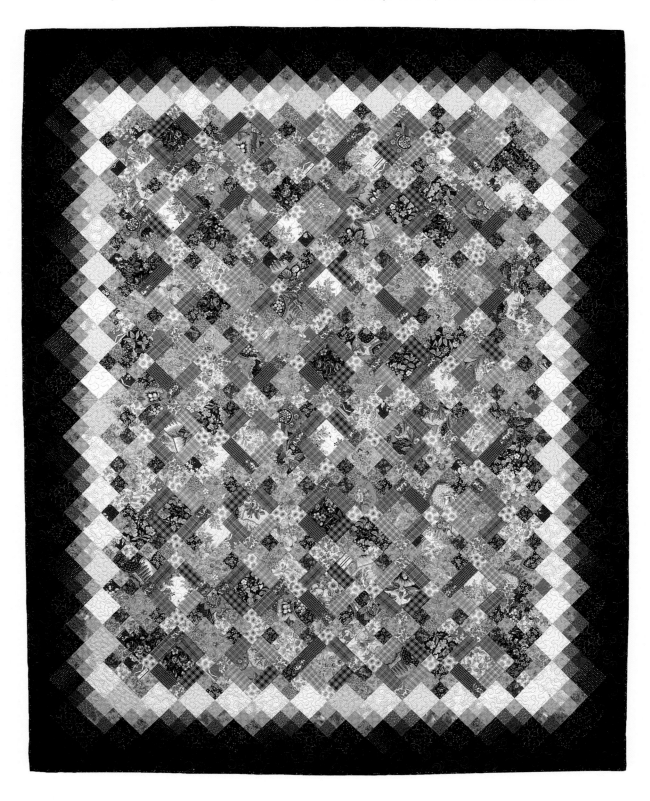

QUILT ESSENTIALS

FINISHED QUILT: 90" x 113" · FINISHED BLOCKS: 16" x 16" · FAT QUARTERS REQUIRED: 62

Clever Fabric Choices: The blended effect in the center of this quilt was achieved through the use of both large-scale and small-scale floral prints combined with plaids—all similar in color and value. The use of beige and black fabrics in the outer blocks and the pieced setting triangles creates the illusion of separate inner and outer borders.

MATERIALS

Yardages are based on 42"-wide fabric.

- 11 fat quarters of assorted large-scale floral prints for blocks
- 11 fat quarters of assorted small-scale floral prints for blocks
- 9 fat quarters of assorted black tone-on-tone prints for outer blocks and setting triangles*
- 7 fat quarters of assorted plaids for blocks
- 2 fat quarters *each* of one black-and-blue print, one black-and-green print, and one black-and-purple print for outer blocks and setting triangles (6 total)*
- 5 fat quarters of assorted beige prints for outer blocks
- 4 fat quarters of assorted accent prints for blocks
- 1 fat quarter *each* of dark blue, dark green, and dark purple tone-on-tone prints for outer blocks and setting triangles (3 total)
- 1 fat quarter *each* of medium blue, medium green, and medium purple tone-on-tone prints for outer blocks and setting triangles (3 total)

- 1 fat quarter *each* of light blue, light green, and light purple tone-on-tone prints for outer blocks and setting triangles (3 total)
- 1 yard of fabric for binding
- 8¼ yards of fabric for backing
- 98" x 121" piece of batting

More than one fat quarter of the same print was included in the assortment.

CUTTING

All measurements include ¼" seam allowances.

From the assorted small-scale floral prints, cut a *total* of:
- 56 strips, 2½" x 21"

From the assorted large-scale floral prints, cut a *total* of:
- 31 strips, 4½" x 21"; cut the strips into 124 squares, 4½" x 4½"

From the assorted plaids, cut a *total* of:
- 20 strips, 4½" x 21". Cut 10 strips into 80 rectangles, 2½" x 4½". Reserve the remaining 10 strips.

From the assorted accent prints, cut a *total* of:

✦ 20 strips, 2½" x 21"

From *each* of the dark blue, dark green, and dark purple tone-on-tone prints, cut:

✦ 3 strips, 2½" x 21" (9 total)

From *each* of the medium blue, medium green, and medium purple tone-on-tone prints, cut:

✦ 6 strips, 2½" x 21" (18 total)

From *each* of the light blue, light green, and light purple tone-on-tone prints, cut:

✦ 3 strips, 2½" x 21" (9 total)

From the assorted beige prints, cut a *total* of:

✦ 14 strips, 4½" x 21"; cut the strips into 56 squares, 4½" x 4½"

From *each* of the 2 black-and-blue fat quarters, cut:

✦ 3 strips, 4½" x 21"; cut the strips into 10 squares, 4½" x 4½" (20 total)

From each of the 2 black-and-green and 2 black-and-purple fat quarters, cut:

✦ 3 strips, 4½" x 21"; cut the strips into 11 squares, 4½" x 4½" (22 squares per color; 44 total)

From the assorted black tone-on-tone prints, cut a *total* of:

✦ 7 squares, 12⅝" x 12⅝"; cut the squares in half diagonally twice to yield 28 triangles

✦ 2 squares, 12¼" x 12¼"; cut the squares in half diagonally once to yield 4 triangles

✦ 8 strips, 4½" x 21"; cut the strips into 32 squares, 4½" x 4½"

ASSEMBLY

1. Randomly sew the 2½"-wide strips cut from the small-scale floral prints into 28 sets of two different strips each. Press the seam allowances toward the darker fabric. Crosscut the strip sets into 224 segments, 2½" wide.

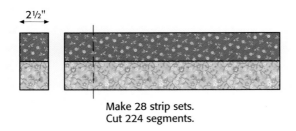

Make 28 strip sets.
Cut 224 segments.

2. Sew the segments from step 1 together as shown to form small four-patch units. Press the seam allowances as desired.

  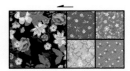

Make 112.

3. Sew a four-patch unit to a large-scale floral square as shown. Make 84. Press the seam allowances toward the floral squares.

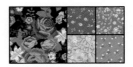

Make 84.

4. Sew the units from step 3 together as shown to make larger four-patch units. Press the seam allowances as desired.

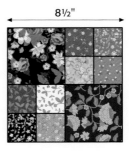

Make 42.

5. Sew the accent-print 2½" x 21" strips to the long edges of the plaid 4½" x 21" strips to make 10 strip sets as shown. Press the seam allowances toward the accent print. Crosscut the strip sets into 80 segments, 2½" wide.

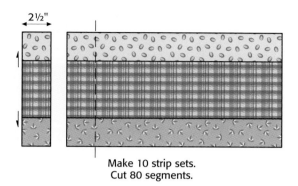

Make 10 strip sets.
Cut 80 segments.

6. Sew the plaid 2½" x 4½" rectangles to opposite sides of the remaining large-scale floral squares. Press the seam allowances toward the squares. Sew the segments from step 5 to the top and bottom of each unit. Press the seam allowances as indicated. Make 40 units.

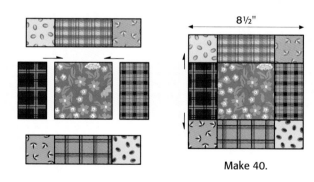

8½"

Make 40.

7. Sew the large four-patch units from step 4 and the units from step 6 together as shown to make 18 inner blocks. Press the seam allowances as indicated.

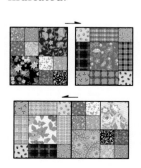

16½"

Inner block.
Make 18.

8. Using the 2½" x 21" strips, sew a medium purple tone-on-tone strip to each light purple and dark purple tone-on-tone strip. Press the seam allowances toward the medium purple. Repeat with the three values of blue and three values of green tone-on-tone prints. Crosscut the strip sets of each color combination into 20 segments, 2½" wide (120 total).

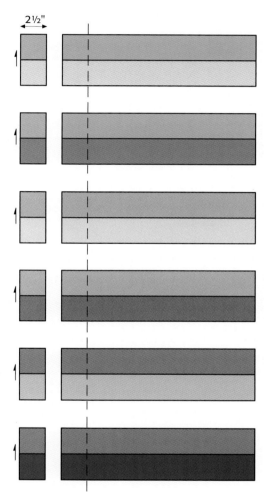

2½"

Make 3 strip sets of each color combination.
Cut 20 segments from each color combination.

9. Sew the segments from step 8 together to make 20 small four-patch units in each of the color combinations shown (60 total). Press the seam allowances as desired.

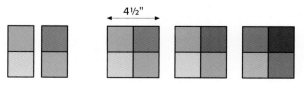

4½"

Make 20 of each color combination.

10. Sew the beige squares, the small four-patch units remaining from step 2, and the small four-patch units from step 9 together as shown to make large four-patch units. Press the seam allowances as indicated.

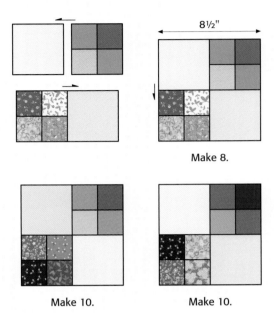

Make 8.

Make 10.   Make 10.

11. Sew the black-and-blue, black-and-green, black-and-purple, and black tone-on-tone squares together with the remaining small four-patch units from step 9 to make large four-patch units as shown. Press the seam allowances as indicated.

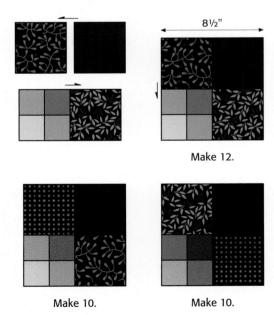

Make 12.

Make 10.   Make 10.

12. Sew the remaining units from steps 4 and 6 and the units from steps 10 and 11 together as shown to make the outer blocks. Press the seam allowances as indicated.

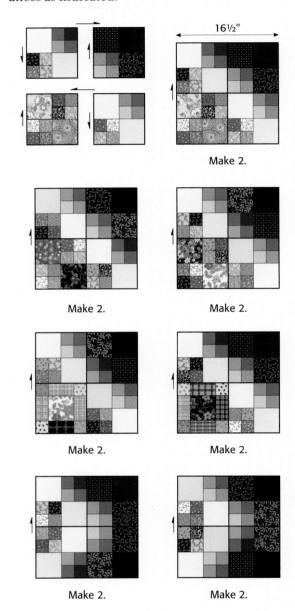

16½"

Make 2.

Make 2.   Make 2.

Make 2.   Make 2.

Make 2.   Make 2.

13. Sew the black tone-on-tone triangles cut from 12⅝" squares to adjacent sides of the remaining units from step 11 to make the setting triangles. Press the seam allowances toward the triangles.

Make 4.

Make 6.

Make 4.

14. Referring to the quilt assembly diagram, sew the blocks, the setting triangles, and the black triangles cut from 12¼" squares together into diagonal rows. Press the seam allowances in opposite directions from row to row. Sew the rows together. Press the seam allowances as desired.

15. Quilt as desired and bind. Refer to "Finishing Your Quilt" on page 17 for details if needed.

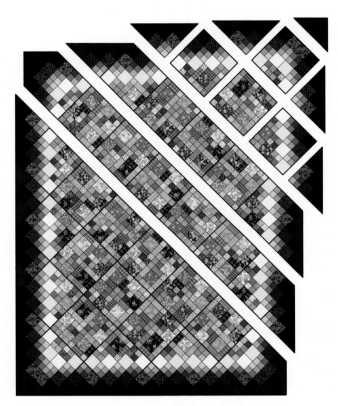

Quilt assembly

CLEVER TIP

Pressing Arrows

By following the pressing arrows throughout the assembly instructions, most seam allowances will be pressed in opposite directions. However, some seam allowances may be pressed in the same direction when the blocks are sewn together into the quilt. If they can't be re-pressed, it's OK to leave them. Just be sure to pin them in place when sewing the blocks together.

Fairy Dust

Designed and sewn by Susan Dissmore; machine quilted by Eileen Peacher, 2005.

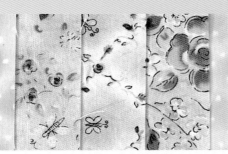
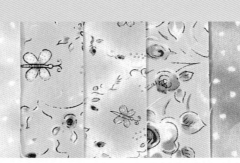
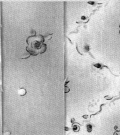

QUILT ESSENTIALS

FINISHED QUILT: 68¼" x 91" · FINISHED BLOCK: 16" x 16" · FAT QUARTERS REQUIRED: 29

Clever Fabric Choices: Sprinkle fairy dust in the room of a special child with this twin-size version of "Floral Foursome" (page 60). The coloring in this quilt speaks "little girl" with soft shades of purple, pink, green, blue, and yellow. To make it speak "little boy" simply change the theme from floral prints to sports (or any other favorite boy theme) and choose colors that coordinate.

MATERIALS

Yardages are based on 42"-wide fabric.

- ✦ 1½ yards of dark purple print for outer blocks and setting triangles
- ✦ 3 fat quarters of assorted medium pink prints for blocks
- ✦ 2 fat quarters *each* of assorted medium green, medium yellow, and medium blue prints for blocks (6 total)
- ✦ 2 fat quarters *each* of assorted green, yellow, and blue floral prints for blocks (6 total)
- ✦ 1 fat quarter *each* of blue, green, pink, and purple plaid for blocks (4 total)
- ✦ 4 fat quarters of assorted beige prints for outer blocks*
- ✦ 4 fat quarters of one medium purple print for outer blocks and setting triangles
- ✦ 2 fat quarters of one light purple print for blocks
- ✦ 5½ yards of fabric for backing
- ✦ ¾ yard of fabric for binding
- ✦ 76" x 99" piece of batting

* More than one fat quarter of the same print was included in the assortment.

CUTTING

All measurements include ¼" seam allowances.

From *each* of the 2 medium green, 2 medium yellow, and 2 medium blue prints, cut:
- ✦ 6 strips, 2½" x 21" (36 total)

From *each* of 2 medium pink prints, cut:
- ✦ 6 strips, 2½" x 21" (12 total)

From the remaining medium pink print, cut:
- ✦ 2 strips, 2½" x 21"

From *each* of the 2 green floral and 2 blue floral prints, cut:
- ✦ 3 strips, 4½" x 21"; cut the strips into 10 squares, 4½" x 4½" (40 total)
- ✦ 1 strip, 2½" x 21" (4 total)

From *each* of the 2 yellow floral prints, cut:
- ✦ 3 strips, 4½" x 21"; cut the strips into 9 squares, 4½" x 4½" (18 total)
- ✦ 1 strip, 2½" x 21" (2 total)

From the light purple print, cut:
- ✦ 12 strips, 2½" x 21"

From *each* of the green and blue plaids, cut:
- ✦ 3 strips, 4½" x 21" (6 total)

From *each* of the pink and purple plaids, cut:

✦ 3 strips, 4½" x 21"; cut the strips into 18 rectangles, 2½" x 4½" (36 total)

From *each* of the 4 beige prints, cut:

✦ 3 strips, 4½" x 21"; cut the strips into 10 squares, 4½" x 4½" (40 total)

From the medium purple print, cut:

✦ 12 strips, 4½" x 21"; cut the strips into 48 squares, 4½" x 4½"

From the dark purple print, cut:

✦ 2 strips, 12⅝" x 42". Cut the strips into 5 squares, 12⅝" x 12⅝"; cut the squares in half diagonally twice to yield 20 triangles.

✦ 1 strip, 12¼" x 42". Cut the strip into 2 squares, 12¼" x 12¼"; cut the squares in half diagonally once to yield 4 triangles.

✦ 3 strips, 4½" x 42"; cut the strips into 24 squares, 4½" x 4½"

ASSEMBLY

1. Sew a medium blue strip to a medium yellow strip to make a strip set. Make 12 strip sets, using the same fabric pairs. Make 2 additional strip sets using the blue floral and yellow floral strips. Press the seam allowances toward the blue. Crosscut the strip sets into 104 segments, 2½" wide. Repeat to make 12 strip sets using the medium green and medium pink strips and 2 strip sets using the green floral and remaining medium pink strips. Press the seam allowances toward the green. Crosscut the strip sets into 104 segments, 2½" wide.

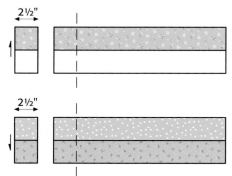

Make 14 strip sets of each color combination (28 total).
Cut 104 segments from each color combination (208 total).

2. Sew a segment from each color combination together as shown to form small four-patch units. Press the seam allowances as desired.

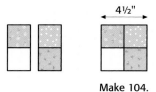

Make 104.

3. Sew a four-patch unit from step 2 to each green floral and blue floral square. Press the seam allowances toward the floral. Sew one of each unit together to make 20 large four-patch units. Press the seam allowances as indicated.

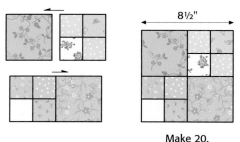

Make 20.

4. Sew the light purple strips to the long edges of each blue plaid strip to make three strip sets. Press the seam allowances toward the light purple. Crosscut the strip sets from each color combination into 18 segments, 2½" wide. Repeat with the green plaid strips and the remaining light purple strips.

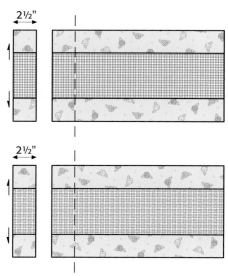

Make 3 strip sets of each color combination (6 total).
Cut 18 segments from each color combination (36 total).

5. Sew the pink plaid and purple plaid rectangles to opposite sides of each yellow floral square. Press the seam allowances toward the squares. Sew the units from step 4 to the top and bottom as shown. Press the seam allowances as indicated.

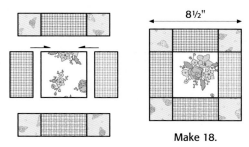

Make 18.

6. Sew the large four-patch units from step 3 and the units from step 5 together as shown to make eight inner blocks. Press the seam allowances as indicated.

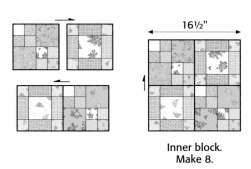

Inner block.
Make 8.

7. Sew the beige squares and small four-patch units from step 2 together as shown to make 20 large four-patch units. Press the seam allowances as indicated.

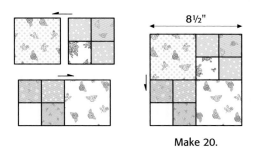

Make 20.

8. Repeat step 7 using the medium purple and dark purple squares and the remaining small four-patch units from step 2 to make 24 large four-patch units. Press the seam allowances as indicated.

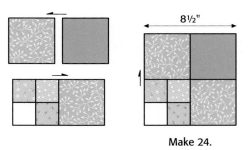

Make 24.

9. Sew the remaining units from steps 3 and 5 and the units from steps 7 and 8 together as shown to make the outer blocks. Press the seam allowances as indicated.

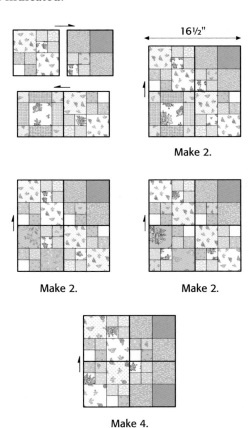

Make 2.

Make 2.   Make 2.

Make 4.

10. Sew the dark purple triangles cut from the 12⅝" squares to each side of the remaining units from step 8 to make the setting triangles. Press the seam allowances toward the triangles.

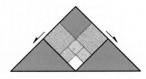

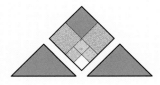

Make 10.

11. Referring to the quilt assembly diagram, sew the blocks, the setting triangles, and the dark purple triangles cut from 12¼" squares together into diagonal rows. Press the seam allowances in opposite directions from row to row. Sew the rows together. Press the seam allowances as desired. (Refer to the pressing tip for "Floral Foursome" on page 65.)

12. Quilt as desired and bind. Refer to "Finishing Your Quilt" on page 17 for details if needed.

Quilt assembly

Petite Foursome

Designed and sewn by Susan Dissmore; machine quilted by Eileen Peacher, 2005.

QUILT ESSENTIALS

FINISHED QUILT: 45" x 56½" · FINISHED BLOCKS: 8" x 8" · FAT QUARTERS REQUIRED: 18

Clever Fabric Choices: This half-size version of "Floral Foursome" (page 60) uses a different color scheme to create a fun baby quilt. Borders in lime green and royal blue frame the center of brightly colored pinks, yellows, purples, blues, and greens.

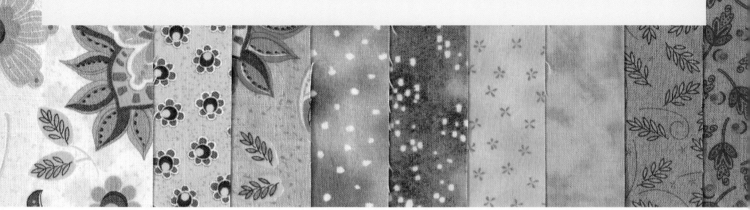

MATERIALS

Yardages are based on 42"-wide fabric.

- ½ yard of dark blue print for blocks and setting triangles
- 2 fat quarters of the same dark green print for blocks
- 2 fat quarters of assorted light prints for blocks
- 2 fat quarters of assorted dark pink prints for blocks
- 2 fat quarters of assorted medium pink prints for blocks
- 2 fat quarters of assorted lavender prints for blocks
- 2 fat quarters of assorted yellow prints for blocks
- 1 fat quarter *each* of blue floral, green floral, and yellow floral print for blocks (3 total)
- 1 fat quarter *each* of light green, medium green, and medium blue prints for blocks and setting triangles (3 total)
- ⅝ yard of fabric for binding
- 3 yards of fabric for backing
- 53" x 65" piece of batting

CUTTING

All measurements include ¼" seam allowances.

From *each* of the 2 medium pink and 2 dark pink prints, cut:

- 9 strips, 1½" x 21" (36 total)

From *each* blue floral print and green floral print, cut:

- 6 strips, 2½" x 21"; cut the strips into 42 squares, 2½" x 2½" (84 total)

From *each* of the 2 yellow prints, cut:

- 7 strips, 1½" x 21". Cut 1 strip into 2 squares, 1½" x 1½" (4 total). Reserve the remaining 6 strips of each print.

From *each* of the 2 lavender prints, cut:

- 6 strips, 2½" x 21". Cut 3 of the strips into 39 rectangles, 1½" x 2½" (78 total). Reserve the remaining 3 strips of each print.
- 1 strip, 1½" x 21"; cut the strip into 2 rectangles, 1½" x 2½" (4 total)

From the yellow floral print, cut:

- 6 strips, 2½" x 21"; cut the strips into 40 squares, 2½" x 2½"

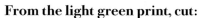

From the light green print, cut:

✦ 5 strips, 1½" x 21"

From the medium green print, cut:

✦ 10 strips, 1½" x 21"

From *each* of the 2 dark green prints, cut:

✦ 4 strips, 2½" x 21"; cut the strips into 32 squares, 2½" x 2½" (64 total)

✦ 3 strips, 1½" x 21" (6 total; 1 extra)

From *each* of the 2 light prints, cut:

✦ 4 strips, 2½" x 21"; cut the strips into 28 squares, 2½" x 2½" (56 total)

From the medium blue print, cut:

✦ 4 strips, 2½" x 21"; cut the strips into 32 squares, 2½" x 2½"

From the dark blue print, cut:

✦ 2 strips, 7" x 42". Cut the strips into 7 squares, 7" x 7"; cut the squares in half diagonally twice to yield 28 triangles.

✦ 2 squares, 6⅝" x 6⅝"; cut the squares in half diagonally once to yield 4 triangles

ASSEMBLY

1. Sew a medium pink strip to a dark pink strip to make a strip set. Make nine strip sets using the same fabric pairs. Press the seam allowances toward the dark pink. Crosscut the strip sets of each fabric combination into 112 segments, 1½" wide. Repeat with the remaining medium pink and dark pink strips.

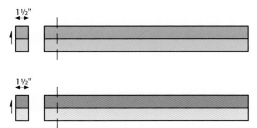

Make 9 strip sets of each fabric combination (18 total).
Cut 112 segments from each fabric combination (224 total).

2. Sew two different segments from step 1 together as shown to make 112 small four-patch units. Press the seam allowances as desired.

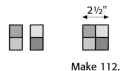

Make 112.

3. Sew a four-patch unit from step 2 to each blue floral and green floral square. Press the seam allowances toward the floral print. Sew one of each unit together to make 42 large four-patch units. Press the seam allowances as desired.

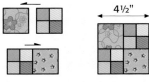

Make 42.

4. Sew matching yellow 1½" x 21" strips to the long edges of a lavender 2½" x 21" strip to make three identical strip sets. Press the seam allowances toward the yellow print. Crosscut the strip sets of each fabric combination into 39 segments, 1½" wide. Repeat with the remaining yellow and lavender strips.

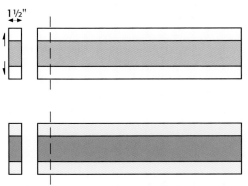

Make 3 strip sets of each fabric combination (6 total).
Cut 39 segments from each fabric combination (78 total).

5. Matching the same prints used in step 4, sew the yellow 1½" squares to each end of the lavender 1½" x 2½" rectangles. Press the seam allowances toward the yellow print.

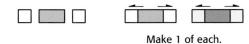

Make 1 of each.

6. Sew matching lavender 1½" x 2½" rectangles to opposite sides of each yellow floral 2½" square. Press the seam allowances toward the squares. Matching the lavender prints, sew the units from steps 4 and 5 to the remaining sides. Press the seam allowances as indicated.

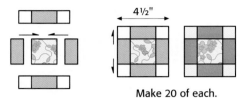

4½"

Make 20 of each.

7. Sew the large four-patch units from step 3 and the units from step 6 together as shown to make 18 inner blocks. Press the seam allowances as indicated.

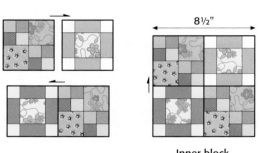

8½"

Inner block.
Make 18.

8. Using the 1½" x 21" strips, sew a medium green strip to each of the five light green strips. Press the seam allowances toward the medium green. Crosscut the strip sets of each color combination into 60 segments, 1½" wide. Repeat with the remaining medium green strips and five dark green strips.

1½"

1½"

Make 5 strip sets of each color combination (10 total).
Cut 60 segments from each color combination (120 total).

9. Sew the segments from step 8 together to make small four-patch units. Press the seam allowances as desired. Make 60 units.

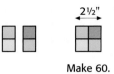

2½"

Make 60.

10. Sew the light-print squares, the small four-patch units from step 2, and the small four-patch units from step 9 together as shown to make 28 large four-patch units. Press the seam allowances as indicated.

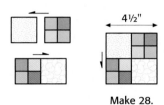

4½"

Make 28.

11. Repeat step 10 using two dark green squares, one medium blue square, and the remaining small four-patch units from step 9 to make 32 large four-patch units. Press the seam allowances as indicated.

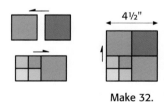

4½"

Make 32.

12. Sew the remaining units from steps 3 and 6 and the units from steps 10 and 11 together as shown to make the outer blocks. Press the seam allowances as indicated.

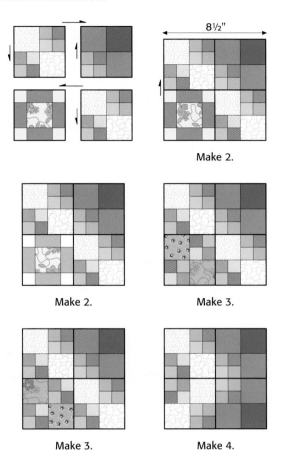

Make 2.

Make 2.   Make 3.

Make 3.   Make 4.

13. Sew the dark blue triangles cut from 7" squares to adjacent sides of each remaining unit from step 11 as shown to make the setting triangles. Press the seam allowances toward the triangles.

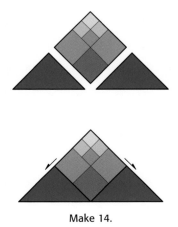

Make 14.

14. Referring to the quilt assembly diagram, sew the blocks, the setting triangles, and the dark blue triangles cut from 6⅝" squares together into diagonal rows. Press the seam allowances in opposite directions from row to row. Sew the rows together. Press the seam allowances as desired. (Refer to the pressing tip for "Floral Foursome" on page 65.)

15. Quilt as desired and bind. Refer to "Finishing Your Quilt" on page 17 for details if needed.

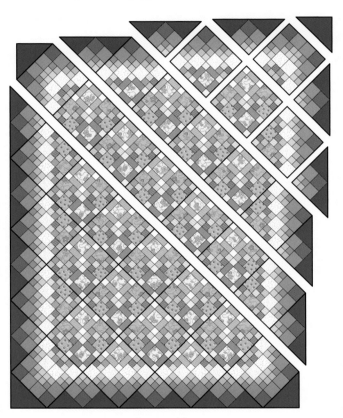

Quilt assembly

Ruby's Golden Railroad

Designed and sewn by Susan Dissmore; machine quilted by Eileen Peacher, 2005.

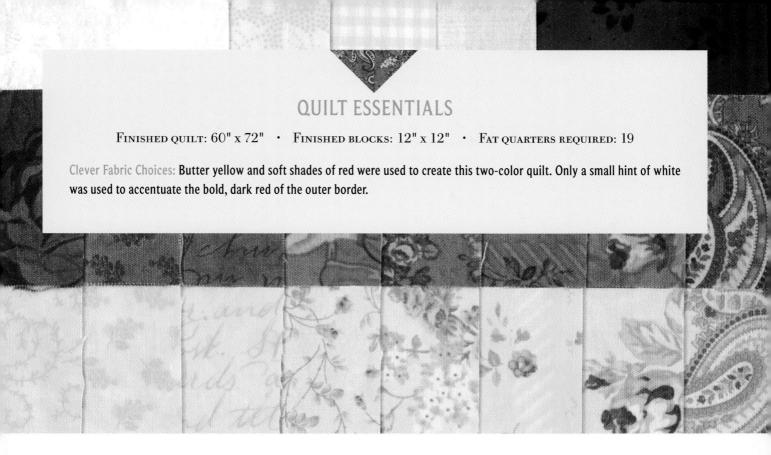

QUILT ESSENTIALS

FINISHED QUILT: 60" x 72" · FINISHED BLOCKS: 12" x 12" · FAT QUARTERS REQUIRED: 19

Clever Fabric Choices: Butter yellow and soft shades of red were used to create this two-color quilt. Only a small hint of white was used to accentuate the bold, dark red of the outer border.

MATERIALS

Yardages are based on 42"-wide fabric.

- 1⅜ yards of dark red print for border blocks
- 5 fat quarters of assorted yellow prints for blocks
- 5 fat quarters of assorted red prints for blocks
- 3 fat quarters of assorted yellow tone-on-tone prints for border blocks
- 3 fat quarters of assorted yellow-and-white prints or checks for border blocks
- 3 fat quarters of assorted red tone-on-tone prints for blocks
- ⅝ yard of white print for border blocks
- ⅝ yard of fabric for binding
- 4 yards of fabric for backing
- 68" x 80" piece of batting

CUTTING

All measurements include ¼" seam allowances.

From *each* of 4 red prints, cut:
- 4 strips, 3⅞" x 21". Cut the strips into 19 squares, 3⅞" x 3⅞"; cut the squares in half diagonally once to yield 38 triangles (152 total).

From the remaining red print, cut:
- 3 strips, 4½" x 21"; cut the strips into 14 rectangles, 3½" x 4½"

From *each* of the 3 red tone-on-tone prints, cut:
- 8 strips, 2" x 21" (24 total; 1 extra)

From *each* of the 5 yellow prints, cut:
- 4 strips, 2" x 21" (20 total)
- 2 strips, 3⅞" x 21". Cut the strips into 10 squares, 3⅞" x 3⅞"; cut the squares in half diagonally once to yield 20 triangles (100 total; 4 extra).

From *each* of the 3 yellow tone-on-tone prints, cut:
- 1 strip, 3" x 21" (3 total)
- 6 strips, 2" x 21" (18 total). Reserve 14 of the strips. Cut the remaining 4 strips into a *total* of:
  - 4 rectangles, 2" x 5"
  - 4 rectangles, 2" x 6½"

From the white print, cut:
- 2 strips, 5⅜" x 42". Cut the strips into 14 squares, 5⅜" x 5⅜"; cut the squares in half diagonally once to yield 28 triangles.
- 1 strip, 5" x 42"; cut the strip into 4 squares, 5" x 5"

From *each* of the 3 yellow-and-white prints or checks, cut:

✦ 2 strips, 7¼" x 21". Cut the strips into 3 squares, 7¼" x 7¼"; cut the squares in half diagonally twice to yield 12 triangles (36 total).

From the dark red print, cut:

✦ 4 strips, 6½" x 42". Cut the strips into:
  - 36 rectangles, 3½" x 6½"
  - 4 squares, 6½" x 6½"
✦ 4 strips, 3⅞" x 42". Cut the strips into 36 squares, 3⅞" x 3⅞"; cut the squares in half diagonally once to yield 72 triangles.

ASSEMBLY

1. Using the triangles cut from 3⅞" squares, sew the red print triangles to the yellow print triangles along their longest edges to make 96 half-square-triangle units. Press the seam allowances toward the red triangles and trim the dog-ears.

Make 96.

2. Using the 2" x 21" strips, sew the red tone-on-tone strips to the yellow print strips as shown to make 20 strip sets. Press the seam allowances toward the red print. Crosscut the strip sets into 192 segments, 2" wide.

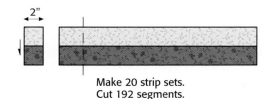

Make 20 strip sets.
Cut 192 segments.

3. Sew the segments from step 2 together as shown to make 96 four-patch units. Press the seam allowances as desired.

Make 96.

4. Sew the units from steps 1 and 3 together as shown. Press the seam allowances as indicated. Make 24 of block A and 24 of block B.

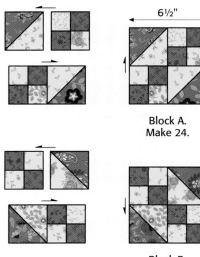

Block A.
Make 24.

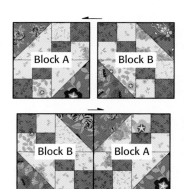

Block B.
Make 24.

5. Sew blocks A and B together as shown to make 12 Railroad Crossing blocks. Press the seam allowances open.

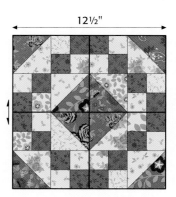

Railroad Crossing block.
Make 12.

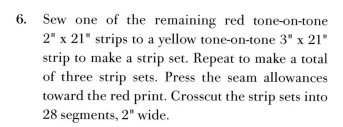

6. Sew one of the remaining red tone-on-tone 2" x 21" strips to a yellow tone-on-tone 3" x 21" strip to make a strip set. Repeat to make a total of three strip sets. Press the seam allowances toward the red print. Crosscut the strip sets into 28 segments, 2" wide.

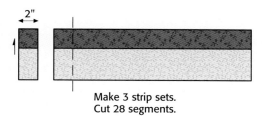

Make 3 strip sets.
Cut 28 segments.

7. Sew the segments from step 6 together into pairs as shown, matching the outside edges. Don't press the seam allowances yet.

Make 14.

8. Clip the seam allowance just through the seam line between the two red squares. Press each side in opposite directions toward the rectangles as shown.

Clip.

9. Line up the 45° line of a ruler along the outer-right edge of the rectangle unit. Draw a diagonal line from the upper-right corner downward through the intersection of the small square seam. Repeat on the left side of the rectangle unit, extending the line upward from the lower-left corner.

10. With right sides together, place each of the marked units from step 9 on a red print 3½" x 4½" rectangle. Sew on the drawn lines, and then cut the units apart between the sewn lines. Press the

seam allowances toward the red print and trim the dog-ears.

Make 28.

11. Sew the remaining red print triangles cut from 3⅞" squares to adjacent sides of each unit from step 10 as shown. Press the seam allowances toward the newly added triangles and trim the dog-ears.

Make 28.

12. With right sides together, sew two of the white triangles cut from 5⅜" squares to one yellow tone-on-tone 2" x 21" strip as shown and leave a 2" gap between the triangles. Press the seam allowances toward the yellow print. Cut the triangles from the strip as shown. Repeat to make a total of 14 units.

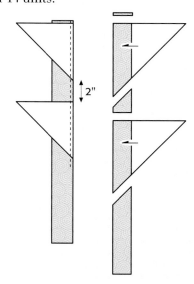

Make 14.

13. Repeat step 12, reversing the position of the triangles as shown.

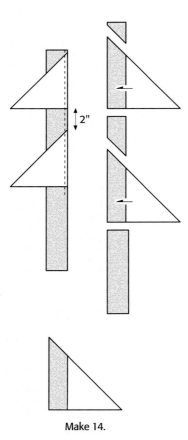

Make 14.

14. Sew the units from steps 11, 12, and 13 together as shown. Press the seam allowances toward the light triangles and trim the dog-ears.

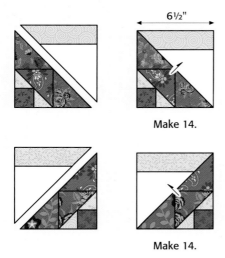

Make 14.

Make 14.

15. Sew a yellow tone-on-tone 2" x 5" rectangle to the top of each white 5" square. Press the seam allowances toward the yellow. Sew the yellow 2" x 6½" rectangles to one side as shown. Press the seam allowances toward the rectangles.

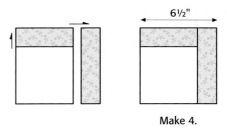

Make 4.

16. Sew the dark red triangles cut from 3⅞" squares to each short side of the yellow-and-white triangles cut from 7¼" squares as shown to make flying-geese units. Press the seam allowances toward the red print and trim the dog-ears.

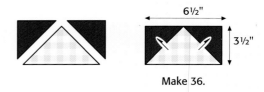

Make 36.

17. Sew a dark red 3½" x 6½" rectangle to the top of each flying-geese unit. Press half of the seam allowances toward the rectangles and the other half toward the flying-geese units.

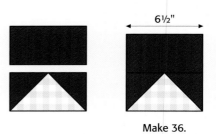

Make 36.

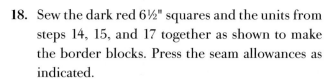

18. Sew the dark red 6½" squares and the units from steps 14, 15, and 17 together as shown to make the border blocks. Press the seam allowances as indicated.

19. Referring to the quilt assembly diagram, sew the Railroad Crossing blocks and border blocks together into rows. Press the seam allowances in opposite directions from row to row. Sew the rows together. Press the seam allowances in one direction.

20. Quilt as desired and bind. Refer to "Finishing Your Quilt" on page 17 for details if needed.

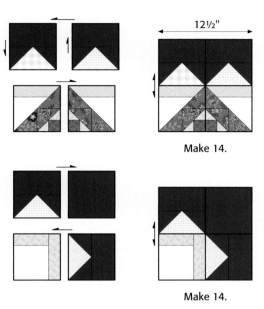

12½"

Make 14.

Make 14.

Quilt assembly

Size Options

Quilt A
Size: 72" x 84"

Quilt B
Size: 84" x 96"

Materials: Multiply each fat quarter amount in the materials list for "Ruby's Golden Railroad" on page 77 by two to determine the amount of fat quarters required. You'll also need ¾ yard of white print and 1⅝ yards of dark red print. Measure the finished quilt to determine the yardage required for the backing and binding, as well as the size of the batting piece.

Materials: Multiply each fat quarter amount in the materials list for "Ruby's Golden Railroad" on page 77 by three to determine the amount of fat quarters required. You'll also need ⅞ yard of white print and 2 yards of dark red print. Measure the finished quilt to determine the yardage required for the backing and binding, as well as the size of the batting piece.

Assembly: Follow the assembly instructions on pages 78–81 for the smaller version, increasing the amount of blocks as shown for each quilt size. If desired, add an additional outer border to increase the size of the finished quilt. Just remember, by adding a border, the amount of yardage required for the backing, binding, and the size of the batting piece will need to be recalculated.

72" x 84": Make 20.
84" x 96": Make 30.

72" x 84": Make 18.
84" x 96": Make 22.

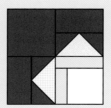

72" x 84": Make 4.
84" x 96": Make 4.

Shining Star Runner

Designed, sewn, and quilted by Susan Dissmore, 2004.

MATERIALS

Yardages are based on 42"-wide fabric.

- 2 fat quarters of the same black print for blocks and setting triangles
- 2 fat quarters of assorted red prints for blocks and setting triangles
- 2 fat quarters of assorted green prints for blocks and setting triangles
- 2 fat quarters of assorted beige prints for blocks
- 1 fat quarter of green striped print for blocks and setting triangles
- $\frac{3}{8}$ yard of fabric for binding
- $1\frac{7}{8}$ yards of fabric for backing
- 23" x 65" piece of batting

CUTTING

All measurements include ¼" seam allowances.

From 1 red print, cut:
- 2 strips, 3¼" x 21". Cut the strips into 8 squares, 3¼" x 3¼"; cut the squares in half diagonally twice to yield 32 triangles.

From *each* of the 2 beige prints, cut:
- 3 strips, 2½" x 21"; cut the strips into 24 squares, 2½" x 2½" (48 total)
- 1 strip, 2⅞" x 21". Cut the strip into 4 squares, 2⅞" x 2⅞"; cut the squares in half diagonally once to yield 8 triangles (16 total).
- 1 strip, 3¼" x 21". Cut the strip into 2 squares, 3¼" x 3¼"; cut the squares in half diagonally twice to yield 8 triangles (16 total).

Clever Fabric Choices: Subtle holiday prints of green, red, and a stripe inspired this seasonal runner. With flexibility in mind, two fat quarters of the same black print were used for the outer border. (Yes, it's OK to use just one print!)

From the green striped print, cut:

✦ 2 strips, 2⅞" x 21". Cut the strips into 12 squares, 2⅞" x 2⅞"; cut 6 of the squares in half diagonally in one direction and the other 6 in half diagonally in the other direction to yield 24 triangles.

✦ 1 strip, 3¼" x 21". Cut the strip into 4 squares, 3¼" x 3¼"; cut the squares in half diagonally twice to yield 16 triangles.

From the black print, cut:

✦ 2 squares, 7" x 7"; cut the squares in half diagonally once to yield 4 triangles

✦ 3 squares, 6⅞" x 6⅞"; cut the squares in half diagonally twice to yield 12 triangles

✦ 4 squares, 2½" x 2½"

From 1 green print, cut:

✦ 6 strips, 2½" x 21"; cut the strips into 16 rectangles, 2½" x 6½"

From the remaining green print, cut:

✦ 4 strips, 2⅞" x 21". Cut the strips into 20 squares, 2⅞" x 2⅞"; cut the squares in half diagonally once to yield 40 triangles.

From the remaining red print, cut:

✦ 10 strips, 1½" x 21". Cut the strips into rectangles in the following order, cutting as many rectangles as you can from one strip before cutting another strip:

  • 4 rectangles, 1½" x 12"

  • 12 rectangles, 1½" x 6"

  • 6 rectangles, 1½" x 5½"

  • 6 rectangles, 1½" x 4½"

ASSEMBLY

1. Using the triangles cut from 3¼" squares, sew a red print triangle to each beige triangle and green striped triangle as shown to make larger triangles. Press the seam allowances toward the red triangles. Sew one of each large triangle together as shown to make quarter-square-triangle units. Press the seam allowances toward the green stripe and trim the dog-ears.

Make 16 of each.

Make 16.

2. Sew four matching beige 2½" squares, four units from step 1, and one black 2½" square together as shown. Press the seam allowances as indicated.

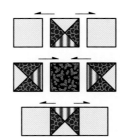 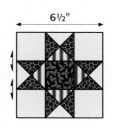

Make 4.

3. With right sides together, place a beige square on one end of a green 2½" x 6½" rectangle. Draw a diagonal line from corner to corner through the beige square as shown. Sew on the diagonal line. Trim ¼" from the stitching line. Press the seam allowances toward the rectangle. Repeat on the opposite end of the green rectangle. Make 16.

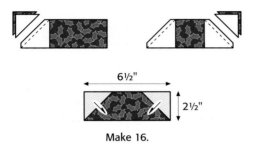

Make 16.

4. Using the triangles cut from 2⅞" squares, sew each beige triangle to a green print triangle along their longest edges to make half-square-triangle units. Press the seam allowances toward the green triangles and trim the dog-ears.

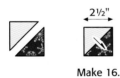

Make 16.

5. Sew the units from steps 2–4 together as shown to make four Star blocks. Press the seam allowances as indicated.

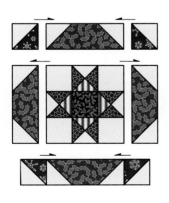

Star block.
Make 4.

6. Repeat step 4 using the green striped triangles and the remaining green print triangles cut from the 2⅞" squares. Press the seam allowances toward the green print triangles and trim the dog-ears.

Make 12.

Make 12.

7. Sew the units from step 6 together as shown to make six pinwheel units. Press the seam allowances as indicated.

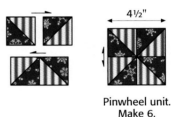

Pinwheel unit.
Make 6.

8. Sew a red 1½" x 4½" rectangle to the bottom of each pinwheel unit. Press the seam allowances toward the red print. Sew a red 1½" x 5½" rectangle to the right-hand side of each unit. Press the seam allowances toward the red print.

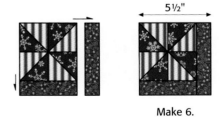

Make 6.

9. Sew a red 1½" x 6" rectangle to one short side of six black triangles cut from the 6⅞" squares as shown. Repeat by sewing a red 1½" x 6" rectangle to the opposite short side of the remaining black triangles. Press the seam allowances toward the triangles. Trim

the red strip even with the long edge of each triangle.

Make 6 of each.

10. Sew the triangle units from step 9 to the red print edges of each pinwheel unit from step 8 as shown to make the side setting triangles. Press the seam allowances toward the triangles and trim the dog-ears.

Side setting triangle.
Make 6.

11. Fold the black triangles cut from 7" squares in half and finger-press to mark the center. Repeat with the red 1½" x 12" rectangles. With the centers aligned, sew a red print strip to the long edge of each triangle to make the corner setting triangles. Press the seam allowances toward the triangles. Trim the red strip even with the short edges of each triangle.

Corner setting triangle.
Make 4.

12. Sew the Star blocks and setting triangles together into diagonal rows. Press the seam allowances in opposite directions from row to row. Sew the rows together. Press the seam allowances as desired. *Note:* The corner setting triangles are slightly larger than necessary. If needed, trim the sides ¼" from the block points.

13. Quilt as desired and bind. Refer to "Finishing Your Quilt" on page 17 for details if needed.

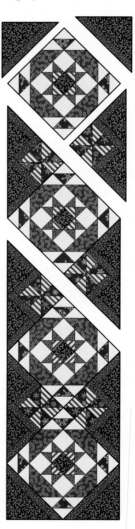

Runner assembly

Shining Star Place Mats

Designed, sewn, and quilted by Susan Dissmore, 2003.

QUILT ESSENTIALS

FINISHED PLACE MAT: 16" x 12"   ·   FINISHED STAR BLOCK: 10" x 10"   ·   FAT QUARTERS REQUIRED: 6

Clever Fabric Choices: The Fourth of July comes to life with these lively red-and-blue place mats. To create the same look, search for any print that feels patriotic. (*Note:* I substituted a flag-print scrap for the two blue print 2½" squares.)

MATERIALS (for 2 place mats)

Yardages are based on 42"-wide fabric.

- ✦ 1 fat quarter of light print for blocks
- ✦ 1 fat quarter of red print for blocks and outer border
- ✦ 1 fat quarter of red tone-on-tone print for inner border
- ✦ 1 fat quarter of blue print for blocks and outer border
- ✦ 1 fat quarter of blue tone-on-tone print for blocks
- ✦ 1 fat quarter (or scrap) of gold for blocks
- ✦ ⅜ yard of fabric for binding
- ✦ ½ yard of fabric for backing
- ✦ 20" x 32" piece of batting

CUTTING (for 2 place mats)

All measurements include ¼" seam allowances.

From the light print, cut:
- ✦ 4 strips, 2½" x 21"; cut the strips into 24 squares, 2½" x 2½"
- ✦ 1 strip, 2⅞" x 21". Cut the strip into 4 squares, 2⅞" x 2⅞"; cut the squares in half diagonally once to yield 8 triangles.
- ✦ 1 strip, 3¼" x 21". Cut the strip into 2 squares, 3¼" x 3¼"; cut the squares in half diagonally twice to yield 8 triangles.

From the gold, cut:
- ✦ 2 squares, 3¼" x 3¼"; cut the squares in half diagonally twice to yield 8 triangles

From the red print, cut:
- ✦ 1 strip, 3¼" x 21". Cut the strip into 4 squares, 3¼" x 3¼"; cut the squares in half diagonally twice to yield 16 triangles.
- ✦ 1 strip, 5¼" x 21". Cut the strip into 3 squares, 5¼" x 5¼"; cut the squares in half diagonally twice to yield 12 triangles.

From the blue tone-on-tone print, cut:
- ✦ 1 strip, 2⅞" x 21". Cut the strip into 4 squares, 2⅞" x 2⅞"; cut the squares in half diagonally once to yield 8 triangles.
- ✦ 3 strips, 2½" x 21"; cut the strips into 8 rectangles, 2½" x 6½"

From the red tone-on-tone print, cut:
- ✦ 8 strips, 1½" x 21". Cut the strips into:
  - • 4 rectangles, 1½" x 10½"
  - • 4 rectangles, 1½" x 12½"

From the blue print, cut:
- ✦ 1 strip, 2⅞" x 21". Cut the strip into 4 squares, 2⅞" x 2⅞"; cut the squares in half diagonally once to yield 8 triangles.
- ✦ 1 strip, 5¼" x 21". Cut the strip into 2 squares, 5¼" x 5¼"; cut the squares in half diagonally twice to yield 8 triangles.
- ✦ 2 squares, 2½" x 2½"

ASSEMBLY

1. Following steps 1–5 on pages 84 and 85 of "Shining Star Runner," make two Star blocks.

2. Sew the red tone-on-tone 1½" x 10½" rectangles to the opposite sides of each Star block. Press the seam allowances toward the red print. Sew the red tone-on-tone 1½" x 12½" rectangles to the top and bottom of each Star block. Press the seam allowances toward the red print.

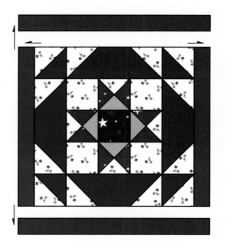

3. Sew three red and two blue triangles cut from 5¼" squares together as shown. Press the seam allowances toward the blue triangles and trim the dog-ears.

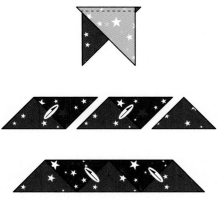

Make 4.

4. Sew the blue print triangles cut from 2⅞" squares to each end of the units from step 3 to complete the outer borders. Press the seam allowances toward the blue triangles.

Make 4.

5. Sew the outer borders to the sides of each place mat top as shown. Press the seam allowances toward the inner borders.

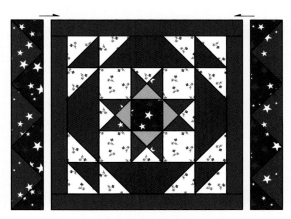

Place mat assembly

6. Quilt as desired and bind. Refer to "Finishing Your Quilt" on page 17 for details if needed.

Summer by the Sea

Designed and sewn by Susan Dissmore; machine quilted by Sue Gantt, 2005.
Inspired by a quilt for the Seaside Rose collection from Moda Fabrics.

QUILT ESSENTIALS

FINISHED RUNNER: 68" x 76½" · FINISHED BLOCKS: 6" x 6" · FAT QUARTERS REQUIRED: 35

Clever Fabric Choices: Dreams of sunshine streaming through the windows of a cottage bedroom adorned with whitewashed furniture, eyelet lace, and fluffy pillows come to mind when looking at this softly colored quilt made with a prebundled collection of fat quarters from the Seaside Rose collection by Moda Fabrics.

MATERIALS

Yardages are based on 42"-wide fabric.

- 6 fat quarters of assorted white floral prints for Half-Square Triangle blocks
- 6 fat quarters of assorted pink prints for Nine Patch blocks
- ⅞ yard of white tone-on-tone print for inner border
- 3 fat quarters *each* of assorted green, aqua, and yellow prints for Nine Patch blocks (9 total)
- 2 fat quarters *each* of assorted pink, green, aqua, and yellow large-scale prints for Half-Square Triangle blocks (8 total)
- 2 fat quarters *each* of assorted pink, green, and aqua tone-on-tone prints for outer border (6 total)
- ¾ yard of fabric for binding
- 5 yards of fabric for backing
- 76" x 84" piece of batting

CUTTING

All measurements include ¼" seam allowances.

From *each* of the 6 assorted pink prints, cut:
- 6 strips, 2½" x 21" (36 total)

From *each* of the 9 assorted green, aqua, and yellow prints, cut:
- 5 strips, 2½" x 21" (45 total)

From *each* of the 6 assorted white floral prints, cut:
- 2 strips, 6⅞" x 21". Cut the strips into 4 squares, 6⅞" x 6⅞"; cut the squares in half diagonally once to yield 8 triangles (48 total; 1 extra from each fabric).
- 1 square, 5⅛" x 5⅛"; cut the square in half diagonally once to yield 2 triangles (12 total)

From *each* of the 8 assorted pink, green, aqua, and yellow large-scale prints, cut:
- 2 strips, 6⅞" x 21". Cut the strips into 4 squares, 6⅞" x 6⅞"; cut the squares in half diagonally once to yield 8 triangles (64 total; 1 extra from each fabric).
- 1 square, 5⅛" x 5⅛"; cut the square in half diagonally once to yield 2 triangles (16 total)

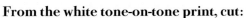

From the white tone-on-tone print, cut:

✦ 3 strips, 6⅞" x 42". Cut the strips into 15 squares, 6⅞" x 6⅞"; cut the squares in half diagonally once to yield 30 triangles.

✦ 1 strip, 5⅛" x 42". Cut the strip into 2 squares, 5⅛" x 5⅛"; cut the squares in half diagonally once to yield 4 triangles.

From *each* of the 2 pink tone-on-tone prints, cut:

✦ 2 squares, 9¾" x 9¾"; cut the squares in half diagonally twice to yield 8 triangles (16 total; 2 extra)

✦ 1 square, 5⅛" x 5⅛"; cut the square in half diagonally once to yield 2 triangles (4 total)

From *each* of the 2 green and 2 aqua tone-on-tone prints, cut:

✦ 1 square, 9¾" x 9¾"; cut the square in half diagonally twice to yield 4 triangles (16 total)

ASSEMBLY

1. Using the 2½" x 21" strips, make six of strip set A and three of strip set B as shown from the pink print and aqua print strips. Press the seam allowances toward the aqua print. Repeat to make strip sets C and D from the pink print and yellow print strips, and strip sets E and F from the pink print and green print strips. Press the seam allowances away from the pink print. Cut each strip set into the number of 2½"-wide segments indicated at right.

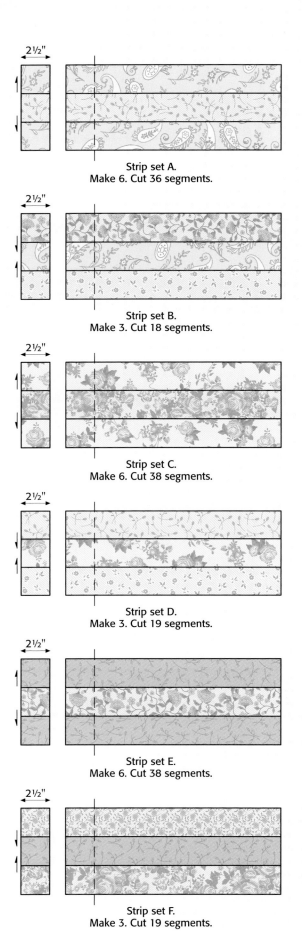

2½"

Strip set A.
Make 6. Cut 36 segments.

2½"

Strip set B.
Make 3. Cut 18 segments.

2½"

Strip set C.
Make 6. Cut 38 segments.

2½"

Strip set D.
Make 3. Cut 19 segments.

2½"

Strip set E.
Make 6. Cut 38 segments.

2½"

Strip set F.
Make 3. Cut 19 segments.

2. Sew the segments together as shown to make the Nine Patch blocks. Press the seam allowances as desired.

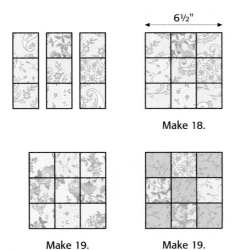

6½"

Make 18.

Make 19.   Make 19.

3. Using the triangles cut from 6⅞" squares, sew the white floral triangles to the pink, green, yellow, and aqua large-scale print triangles along their longest edges to make the Half-Square Triangle blocks as shown. Press the seam allowances toward the darker fabric and trim the dog-ears.

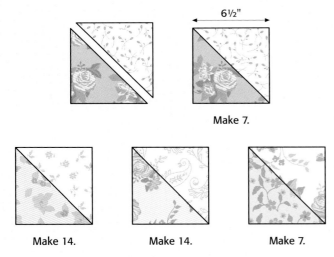

6½"

Make 7.

Make 14.   Make 14.   Make 7.

4. Repeat step 3 using the white tone-on-tone triangles and the remaining green and aqua triangles cut from the 6⅞" squares.

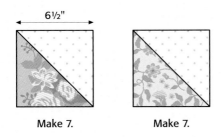

6½"

Make 7.   Make 7.

5. Using the triangles cut from 5⅛" squares, sew the white floral triangles to the aqua, green, yellow, and pink large-scale print triangles to make larger triangle units as shown. Press the seam allowances toward the darker fabric.

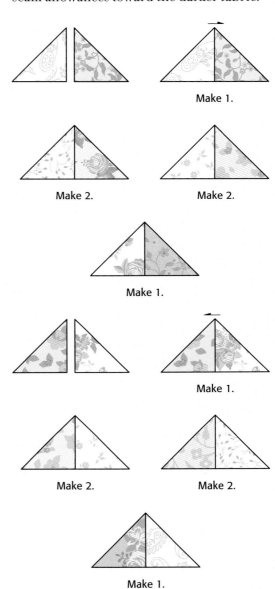

Make 1.

Make 2.   Make 2.

Make 1.

Make 1.

Make 2.   Make 2.

Make 1.

6. Repeat step 5 using the white tone-on-tone triangles and the remaining green and aqua triangles cut from the 5⅛" squares.

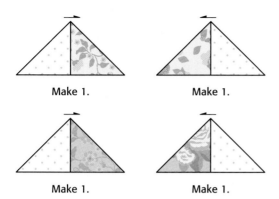

Make 1. Make 1.

Make 1. Make 1.

7. Sew the remaining white tone-on-tone triangles cut from 6⅞" squares to the units from steps 5 and 6 to make the border blocks. Press the seam allowances toward the white triangles and trim the dog-ears.

8. Sew the blocks; the pink, green, and aqua tone-on-tone triangles cut from 9¾" squares; and the pink tone-on-tone triangles cut from 5⅛" squares together in diagonal rows. Press the seam allowances toward the Half-Square Triangle blocks and border blocks.

9. Quilt as desired and bind. Refer to "Finishing Your Quilt" on page 17 for details if needed.

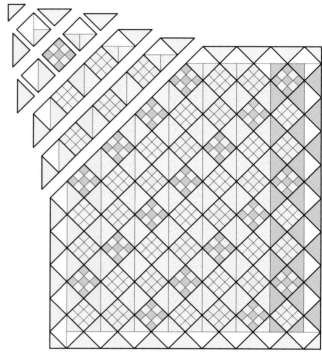

Quilt assembly

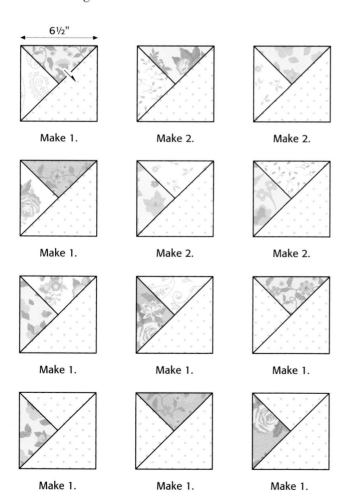

6½"

Make 1. Make 2. Make 2.

Make 1. Make 2. Make 2.

Make 1. Make 1. Make 1.

Make 1. Make 1. Make 1.

About the Author

Susan Teegarden Dissmore

Susan Teegarden Dissmore was taught to sew as a teenager growing up in eastern Washington. It wasn't until late 1994 (after opening a fabric shop) that she learned how to quilt. She soon began designing her own quilts, which gave her much delight. Her favorite quilts are scrap quilts that typically incorporate a multitude of fat quarters. She is a nonpracticing certified public accountant and lives in Federal Way, Washington, with her husband, Tim. They have two sons, Blake and Justin.

New and Bestselling Titles from

America's Best-Loved Craft & Hobby Books
America's Best-Loved Knitting Books

America's Best-Loved Quilt Books

NEW RELEASES
Adoration Quilts
Better by the Dozen
Blessed Home Quilt, The
Hooked on Wool
It's a Wrap
Let's Quilt!
Origami Quilts
Over Easy
Primitive Gatherings
Quilt Revival
Sew One and You're Done
Scraps of Time
Simple Chenille Quilts
Simple Traditions
Simply Primitive
Surprisingly Simple Quilts
Two-Block Theme Quilts
Wheel of Mystery Quilts

APPLIQUÉ
Appliqué Takes Wing
Easy Appliqué Samplers
Garden Party
Raise the Roof
Stitch and Split Appliqué
Tea in the Garden

LEARNING TO QUILT
Happy Endings, Revised Edition
Loving Stitches, Revised Edition
Magic of Quiltmaking, The
Quilter's Quick Reference Guide, The
Your First Quilt Book (or it should be!)

PAPER PIECING
40 Bright and Bold Paper-Pieced Blocks
50 Fabulous Paper-Pieced Stars
300 Paper-Pieced Quilt Blocks
Easy Machine Paper Piecing
Quilt Block Bonanza
Quilter's Ark, A
Show Me How to Paper Piece

PIECING
40 Fabulous Quick-Cut Quilts
101 Fabulous Rotary-Cut Quilts
365 Quilt Blocks a Year: Perpetual
    Calendar
1000 Great Quilt Blocks
Big 'n Easy
Clever Quilts Encore
Once More around the Block
Stack a New Deck

QUILTS FOR BABIES & CHILDREN
American Doll Quilts
Even More Quilts for Baby
More Quilts for Baby
Quilts for Baby
Sweet and Simple Baby Quilts

SCRAP QUILTS
More Nickel Quilts
Nickel Quilts
Save the Scraps
Successful Scrap Quilts
    from Simple Rectangles
Treasury of Scrap Quilts, A

TOPICS IN QUILTMAKING
Alphabet Soup
Cottage-Style Quilts
Creating Your Perfect Quilting Space
Focus on Florals
Follow the Dots . . . to Dazzling Quilts
More Biblical Quilt Blocks
Scatter Garden Quilts
Sensational Sashiko
Warm Up to Wool

CRAFTS
Bag Boutique
Purely Primitive
Scrapbooking Off the Page…
    and on the Wall
Stamp in Color
Vintage Workshop, The: Gifts for All
    Occasions

KNITTING & CROCHET
200 Knitted Blocks
365 Knitting Stitches a Year: Perpetual
    Calendar
Crochet from the Heart
First Crochet
First Knits
Fun and Funky Crochet
Handknit Style
Knits from the Heart
Little Box of Knitted Ponchos and Wraps,
    The
Little Box of Knitted Throws, The
Little Box of Crocheted Hats and Scarves,
    The
Little Box of Scarves, The
Little Box of Scarves II, The
Little Box of Sweaters, The
Pursenalities
Sensational Knitted Socks

Our books are available at bookstores and your favorite craft,
fabric, and yarn retailers. If you don't see the title
you're looking for, visit us at
www.martingale-pub.com
or contact us at:

1-800-426-3126

International: 1-425-483-3313 **Fax:** 1-425-486-7596
Email: info@martingale-pub.com